THE LAST PHARAOH
and Other Plays

Wagdi Zeid

THE LAST PHARAOH
and Other Plays

iUniverse, Inc.
Bloomington

The Last Pharaoh and Other Plays

iUniverse books may be ordered through booksellers or by contacting:

iUniverse
1663 Liberty Drive
Bloomington, IN 47403
www.iuniverse.com
1-800-Authors (1-800-288-4677)

ISBN: 978-1-4759-5201-8 (sc)
ISBN: 978-1-4759-5202-5 (hc)
ISBN: 978-1-4759-5203-2 (e)

Library of Congress Control Number: 2012918031

Printed in the United States of America

iUniverse rev. date: 9/25/2012

For UMass Provost, Professor Ahmed Abdelal,
whose exceptional success in academia has been a case study
for the Harvard Institutes Of Higher Education

The Last Pharaoh: A Play in Two Acts

CHARACTERS

AKHNATON	Pharaoh of Egypt
NEFERTITI	Akhnaton's wife
MERRY	Their daughter
TYE	Akhnaton's mother
ZEMAT	Nefertiti's sister
HOREMOHEB	Zemat's husband, general of the Egyptian armies
HIGH PRIEST OF AMON	
THIRD PRIEST OF AMON	
SECOND PRIEST OF AMON	
FIRST PRIEST OF AMON	
A PRIEST	
MAHU	Chief of police
TOTO	Chief of security
MERORA	A commoner
BEK	Master sculptor and architect
TARA SISTERS	
OLD WOMAN	
YOUNG MAN	
PEASANT MEN, WOMEN, and CHILDREN	
SOLDIERS and GUARDS	
VILLAGERS	

3

ACT ONE

SCENE ONE

(The court of a temple in a village on the bank of the River Nile. Villagers are gathered around a frightened, skinny boy carrying a small sack of grain. A plump, stormy priest paces up and down, glancing fiercely at the boy, whose fear mounts every time the priest gets close to him. Like the boy, the villagers have scraggy, tired figures. Disguised among the villagers stand Akhnaton and two guards, closely following what is going on.)

PRIEST, *moving upstage and turning to his audience.* A sack of grain is nothing, folks. But it is just a beginning! *(He pauses and then screams his next line.)* It is a beginning, and gods know what is next! *(He moves downstage toward the boy; stops right in front of him, looking into his eyes; and then returns.)* Shall we wait, folks? Shall we wait to see him steal more and teach other children to steal? Shall we wait?

(Silence)

Shall we wait till we have all our kids thieves like him? Of course not! No! I can hear everybody here say no! (Looks suspiciously toward the three disguised figures.) But you should know that it was the devil that made him steal. Therefore (glancing at one of his followers) we will punish the devil in him!

(The follower moves toward the boy, takes off his shirt, and leads him toward the center, where he will be whipped.)

AKHNATON, *stepping toward the priest.* Did you ask the boy why?

PRIEST, *turning to Akhnaton violently.* Excuse me, I didn't hear you.

5

AKHNATON. Did you ask the boy why he did what he did?

PRIEST, *moving downstage toward Akhnaton after a moment of silence.* Who are you? I haven't seen you here before.

AKHNATON, *calmly.* I am asking—Did you ask the boy why he stole a sack of grain?

PRIEST, And I am asking, Who are you?

AKHNATON, *removing his cloak, still calmly.* Akhnaton.

(*Akhnaton is thin and feeble. His clothes are simple, and his appearance calls more for pity than admiration. His face is lined with worry, and in his sad eyes one recognizes the hunted look that tells of a searching spirit. Seeing him for the first time creates a sense of disappointment. But the sense of disappointment is only momentary; one gradually becomes charmed by his warm, inspiring presence.*)

PRIEST, *confused.* Who?

AKHNATON. I am Akhnaton, the king of Egypt!

(*Completely dumbfounded, the priest and villagers gaze at Akhnaton in fear and disbelief!*)

PRIEST, *trying to control his fear.* No, no, you are not. It cannot be!

AKHNATON, *glancing at the guards, who reveal themselves and move toward the boy to release him.* Did you ask him why?

BOY, *crying.* We have nothing to eat. Mum is sick and Dad is dead.

AKHNATON, *to the priest after a pause.* What can you say now? What can your blind and deaf gods say now? What can your blind and deaf gods do now?

(*Silence*)

AKHNATON, *to the two guards.* Go inside and destroy the idols of their blind and deaf gods. Let us see what they can say or do.

(The two guards quickly disappear inside the temple. Now, loud sounds of idols being destroyed are heard. The priest stands confounded and helpless. People start to kneel down in fear.)

AKHNATON. Do not kneel down to me. I am not a god! I am only a human being and you shouldn't kneel down to a human being like you! You do not kneel to anyone. There are no gods on earth!

(Blackout)

Scene Two

(A hall in Akhnaton's palace in Tel el Amarna, the city of light. Enter Akhnaton and Tye, his mother. He seems to be in a good mood, but she looks worried.)

AKHNATON. I'm glad, Mother, you changed your mind. You'll like it here. I'm sure you'll like your palace. You'll like this fair city—

TYE, *interrupting.* Look, Son. I'm tired, and I feel I've only a few days to live. I'm here for one thing, and you know it, Son.

AKHNATON. What?

TYE. I'm worried about you. You came to Thebes for the burial of your father and didn't even wait for the seventy days of the embalming. You came back here, and I know what you're going to do! *(Pleading)* Son ... *(She hesitates, stops.)*

AKHNATON, *smiling, encouraging.* I'm listening, Mother.

TYE. I've seen your father rule this empire for thirty-seven years, and I know the Egyptians. You're now the pharaoh of Egypt. You're alone on the throne now.

AKHNATON, *calmly.* I've never really been on the throne, Mother.

TYE. You coruled with him for thirteen years.

AKHNATON, *tenderly.* You know quite well that isn't true, Mother. He never allowed me to do what I really wanted and ... *(Stops.)*

TYE. Because of your ideas!

AKHNATON. My ideas? Corrupt flatterers made him believe he was the greatest pharaoh and he had to build a fourth pyramid bigger than the other three. So for years we have been wasting the country on a

8

huge tomb. We have wasted everything, and it is not yet finished. *(He pauses. Then, in a determined, threatening tone)* And it will never be finished.

TYE. What do you mean?

AKHNATON. You know what I mean. You're talking about my ideas … *(Pauses.)* I've been away the last two years building this simple city. Here is my beginning. The change will start from here. I am not going to build a pyramid for myself, but I will help every Egyptian to be himself a pyramid! The change will start from here, Mother.

TYE, *almost screaming.* They wouldn't allow you!

AKHNATON. Who wouldn't allow me?

TYE. You know—them.

AKHNATON. The priests?

TYE. The priests and their followers. Their followers are all the Egyptians. *(Pauses, comes to him, holds his hand, pleading.)* I see horrible dreams. I … I … *(Stops, trying to control herself, and turns away as if recalling the dream. Then, in a scared, weak voice)* No, no. I don't want to lose you.

(Silence)

AKHNATON, *going to her, holding both her hands with emotion.* Where's the courageous queen who stood beside her king for long years? *(Takes her to the center of the stage. Then, after a pause)* What worries you, Mother? Tell me what you want.

TYE. Learn the wisdom of your father and grandfathers.

AKHNATON. What wisdom?

TYE. Don't confront the priests and their gods.

Akhnaton, *calmly.* My God commands me that no other deity should be worshipped in his land. *(A pause as he looks into her eyes with emotion)* Mother, you believe me?

Tye. You've never lied to me.

Akhnaton. Mother, Father allowed me to be on the throne with him the last few years before his death—did it work? No, it didn't work! And you know it didn't!

Tye. You cannot hold him solely responsible!

Akhnaton. It is not him or me! It's both of us. It didn't work, and it will never work, because you cannot have two rulers for Egypt! If it does not work for Egypt, it does not work for the world! The world should have one God! It does not need a prophet to know it, Mother! *(Pauses.)* You believe in the one and only God?

Tye. I said you've never lied to me.

Akhnaton. This isn't the answer to my question.

(Silence)

Tye, *drawing nearer.* Give yourself time.

Akhnaton. I want to begin right.

Tye. There's no rush. Wisdom—

Akhnaton, *interrupting.* Mother, you said my father and grandfathers were wise and didn't confront the priests and their gods. What was the outcome? Every village now has its own god. Temples have become a huge business, and the priests' pockets grow fat every day while the people suffer.

Tye. Don't face all of them at the same time then. *(Ponders.)* Or at least don't face the high priest of Amon, Riptah. That man has brains, vision, and courage.

Akhnaton. I'm not afraid. My God will not forsake me.

TYE. Find a way to exclude him from the confrontation.

AKHNATON. No compromise, Mother.

(*Tye moves slowly toward a couch, murmuring.*)

(*Blackout*)

SCENE THREE

(A street in Tel el Amarna. Music is heard from afar. Peasant men, women, and children are looking upward in the direction of the music and lights of a festival offstage. The children are very attracted and start to move toward the festival, but their parents do not allow them. Despite the festive atmosphere, parents' faces and movements reveal tension and fear. Downstage left and right, the First Priest of Amon, the Second Priest of Amon, and three guards, all disguised in cloaks, are watching the people impatiently. The two priests have shaved heads and wear shoes of papyrus. While they watch the crowd and exchange looks of obvious indignation, the three guards stand ready. Two boys enter and play festal games like wrestling, boxing, and single-stick fencing. Then they move upstage toward the festival. Children follow them, trying to free their hands from their parents' grip. Looking at the two priests and the three guards in fear, the parents are reluctant to let them go.)

FATHER, *firmly holding his boy's hand.* No. I said no.

CHILD, *begging, trying to escape his father's grip.* Please, Papa, I want to go. Let me go, please.

FATHER. I said no. No. Do you understand?

CHILD. Please, Papa, I want to see the new pharaoh.

FATHER. No.

MOTHER. Can't you let the boy go like other kids?

FATHER, *looking in fear and suspicion at the priests.* Shut up, woman. You know nothing.

MOTHER. Let him go see the festival!

FATHER. Festivals or no festivals, we have to keep away. *(Pauses.)* Every silver lining has a cloud!

CHILD, *almost yelling.* Let me go, Papa!

FATHER, *angrily.* Shut up! Shut up!

OLD MAN, *interfering.* Hey, don't do that to your kid, son!

FATHER. Mind your own business, sir.

OLD MAN. Son, kids are kids. You need—

FATHER, *amazed.* This is my boy, sir, and I need nobody to tell me how to handle him.

OLD MAN, *smiling.* I'm not saying you don't know how to handle him, son. *(Unaware of the presence of the priests and the three guards, he approaches the child and kneels gently.)* You want to see the new pharaoh? You will. I also want to see Akhnaton, the new pharaoh. But we have to wait a few days more.

CHILD. How many?

OLD MAN. Can you count three days? *(Holds the boy's hand to count.)* The crowning festival will be in three days. Tomorrow is one. Then …

CHILD, *happily.* Two and three!

OLD MAN. The third day is the big day of the festival. The new pharaoh will be crowned on that day.

(The First Priest glances at the First Guard, who moves toward the Old Man and stops right behind him.)

OLD MAN, *still unaware.* On that day, son, you'll have a lot of sweets. You, your father and mother, and your friends will see the new pharaoh. You'll see a pharaoh who is completely different from those before him. He is—

FIRST GUARD, *fiercely.* You talk too much.

OLD MAN, *stunned and scared.* I'm only—

FIRST GUARD. Stop it. I don't want to hear more talk. Get home. *(Pushes him violently.)* Go home!

(The Old Man exits. The guard gets back to where he was, glaring at the others threateningly.)

FATHER, *to his child and wife.* I told you. I knew.

FIRST GUARD, *sharply.* What was that you said?

FATHER. Nothing. *(Looks at the sky.)* I said it looks like rain. *(Turning to his wife and child)* Let's get home.

(The three exit. The guard is still glaring at the crowd. Tension and fear increase.)

MAN, looking at the sky, trying to show he is not scared. It seems we'll have a lot of rain. Besides, it's getting cold. Very cold, indeed! *(Pauses. Then, to the others, convincingly)* Home is sweet now, isn't it?

(The crowd disperse toward their homes.)

SECOND PRIEST. Time servers! Cowards!

FIRST PRIEST. Ignorant hypocrites!

(Silence. Another group of commoners, led by a young man who carries images of the new pharaoh, appears. The Second Guard bars their way to the festival.)

SECOND GUARD. Where are you going? *(To the Young Man)* Why do you lead these men about the streets?

YOUNG MAN. Why?

SECOND GUARD, *hitting him with a rod on his shoulder.* I'm the one asking. You don't ask. *(Hits him again.)* Why do you lead these idle creatures about the streets?

(The Young Man violently tries to kick back, but the Third Guard strikes him from behind.)

YOUNG MAN. Why? Why do you do this to us? We're not slaves.

FIRST GUARD, *hitting him again on the shoulder.* Don't give me this crap.

SECOND GUARD, *snatching the images from the Young Man.* What's this? *(Looks at the images and hands them to the First Priest, who also looks at them and then hands them to the Second Priest.)*

YOUNG MAN, *confused but steadfast.* Images of the new pharaoh? And we're going to the festival around the temple ... Is something wrong with this?

(Guards and priests exchange quick, meaningful looks.)

SECOND PRIEST, *stepping toward the Young Man calmly.* Look, young man, you seem to belong to a good family. Who is your father?

YOUNG MAN. Nakht Khamu.

SECOND PRIEST, *writing down the name, trying to remember.* Nakht Khamu ... from Dekma?

YOUNG MAN. Yes.

SECOND PRIEST. Your family is a big one in the area. *(Pauses, thinking.)* Dekma is in the Middle Delta, a long way from here. Why should you come this long way and get involved in suspicious matters?

YOUNG MAN. Suspicious matters! I'm here with my friends to attend the coronation of the new pharaoh, Akhnaton, and the images in your hand are his. We—

SECOND PRIEST, *interrupting sharply.* No, these are not the images of the pharaoh. A pharaoh wouldn't dress like ordinary people. *(Pauses.)* Who gave you these images?

YOUNG MAN. I don't know.

SECOND PRIEST, *glancing at the First Guard.* Take him!

(*The First Guard rudely collars the Young Man, forcing him offstage.*)

YOUNG MAN, *screaming while exiting.* I'm a teacher. You can't do this to me!

SECOND PRIEST, *turning to the Young Man's comrades, in a threatening tone.* And you!

(*They look too scared to speak.*)

SECOND PRIEST, *after a pause.* Get back to your village now. Be gone!

(*They flee.*)

SECOND PRIEST, *to the Second Guard.* Go down that street toward the temple. (*Then, to the Third Guard*) You take the other street. Drive away the ignorant hypocrites from the streets. Remove the heretic's images and let nobody carry them.

(*The two guards exit. Silence. Music is no longer heard. The stage is dark, but the two priests can be dimly seen. The Second Priest moves thoughtfully upstage and then turns to the First Priest.*)

SECOND PRIEST. Go see how the guards carry out the orders. Trust nobody.

FIRST PRIEST. And you?

SECOND PRIEST. Our lord the high priest will arrive from Thebes before midnight, and I have a word from him to our man in the court. Go now, and trust nobody as I said. Don't forget—we meet at midnight behind the temple.

(*Blackout*)

Scene Four

(*Behind one of Tel el Amarna's temples. Midnight. Thunder and lightning. Enter the Second Priest with the images in his hand, followed by the First Priest. They are still disguised in cloaks.*)

Second Priest, *looking around.* A safe place!

First Priest. Yes.

Second Priest, *looking at the sky.* The southern star has appeared. The flood will be bad this year!

First Priest. Yes.

Second Priest. The river is beginning to burst its banks! (*Taking off his cloak*) We're lucky all our men arrived before it got worse.

First Priest, *taking off his cloak after a pause.* Does our lord know how to get here?

Second Priest. He's coming with Soka. Hush—I hear voices.

(*Enter the High Priest and the Third Priest. They are also disguised in cloaks.*)

Second Priest, running to meet the High Priest. My lord, our holy father. (*Kneels, kisses his hand.*) Thank the gods you've arrived safe and well!

First Priest, *kneeling, kissing his hand.* My lord.

High Priest. It was a long, tiring way.

(*He takes off his cloak, and then the Third Priest does likewise. The High Priest looks tired and deeply concerned. He is an elderly man with a shaved head. He is dressed in a long, flowing skirt with a black*

17

sash wrapped around his shoulders and chest. Despite his age, he is a man of vigor, with a powerful body and features revealing quiet confidence; a cruel, hidden force; and cunning.)

SECOND PRIEST. How is Thebes, my lord?

HIGH PRIEST. One more of our temples was destroyed when the heretic came for the king's funeral.

THIRD PRIEST, *morbidly.* He couldn't wait the seventy days for embalming his father's body!

SECOND PRIEST, *angrily.* And the people, my lord?

HIGH PRIEST. Torn between their loyalty to their gods and their obligation to the royal family! *(Pauses.)* But our gods turn things to their own ends. Where's Toto?

SECOND PRIEST. He said he would come a few minutes late.

THIRD PRIEST, *carefully.* We should count on nobody but ourselves. I mean, do you trust Toto, my lord?

HIGH PRIEST. Yes, I do. You should trust those who would do anything for their ambition. Years ago, Toto came to me and reported about his own brother. Therefore, I planted him in the royal court.

FIRST PRIEST, *amazed.* He betrayed his own brother?

THIRD PRIEST. He can betray anybody then!

HIGH PRIEST, *calmly.* Only if you don't give him what he wants. We've given him a lot, and we still have more he wants. I trust him because I know his price.

(Enter Toto. He has a fleshy face with bulging eyes, and his ill temper can be easily recognized.)

HIGH PRIEST. Here comes our great friend. Welcome, Toto!

TOTO, *kneeling, kissing his hand.* My lord.

HIGH PRIEST, *reading his face.* You've got news, Toto?

TOTO. Bad news, my lord!

HIGH PRIEST. What?

TOTO. The prince issued some orders he will declare himself on the crowning day.

HIGH PRIEST. What orders?

TOTO. From that day forth, official temple worship shall cease. The names of Amon and of all other gods shall be erased, and the priesthood shall be dispossessed. Every idol shall be annihilated!

(All are stunned.)

HIGH PRIEST, *still calmly.* You said he issued those orders?

TOTO. Yes, he did. He will declare that a new God has revealed himself to the crown prince claiming to be the one and only true God and that all other gods are fake!

FIRST PRIEST. Our gods are fake!

(Silence)

THIRD PRIEST. Something should be done, my lord, and before he is crowned. Day one after the crowning, he will destroy all our temples and then turn on us, the priests of Amon and other gods.

SECOND PRIEST. He will deprive us of our lands.

FIRST PRIEST. Our houses and wives!

THIRD PRIEST, *moving toward the High Priest.* What else we are waiting for, my lord? More humiliation?

HIGH PRIEST, *avoiding their urging looks, pacing about, calmly turning to them.* Don't panic, friends. *(Moves toward the Third Priest.)* I admire your courage, Soka. However, if you're going to lead the priests of Egypt someday, always keep your vision clear so you can discover the ways of the gods.

THIRD PRIEST. But we're wasting time, my lord.

HIGH PRIEST, *fiercely*. No, we aren't. *(Pauses.)* I expected all this. The prince is a young fool. I knew he would rush things. But this will be for our benefit.

THIRD PRIEST. How?

HIGH PRIEST. Our gods have been engrained in the hearts and minds of the people for thousands of years, and this impatient dreamer cannot change that. *(Looks around, glances at a ladder by the wall, moves toward it.)* Egypt is in our hands. *(Holds the ladder against the wall, referring to it.)* We're on top and everywhere. The prince has never really been anywhere here. *(Gesturing to the top of the ladder)* His father stayed here for thirty-seven years and never trusted him because he knew him. Even when the king fell seriously ill in the last two years, he forced his son to leave Thebes instead of allowing him to rule. *(Moves away from the wall.)* He came to this wilderness to build his city. But we will not allow him to finish what he started. I promise you, friends, what he has built will be ashes soon. *(Pauses.)* Toto!

TOTO. I'll be the first to strike—

HIGH PRIEST, *interrupting*. No, we're not there yet. We were ready for the confrontation in Thebes. But the young fool has made our job easier. *(Then, decisively)* We will defeat him here. *(Pauses.)* We have a lot of work before the crowning. *(To Toto)* We need to know about every move in the court. Keep an eye on Horemoheb and Merora, your rival.

TOTO. I'll do that, my lord.

HIGH PRIEST, *to the priests*. We have a lot of underground work to do among the people in the streets!

SECOND PRIEST, *showing him the images*. We found these images with a young man a few hours ago.

Toto, *looking with the High Priest at the images.* The same funny clothes he wears. He goes to villages on the other side of the Nile disguised in these clothes!

High Priest. Why?

Toto. I don't know.

High Priest, *eagerly.* Do people recognize him?

Toto. No.

High Priest, *satisfied.* Good. *(A pause. Then, to the Second Priest)* What did you do to the young man?

Second Priest. We took him to one of our caves in the mountain.

High Priest. Don't release him till we're done. Have our men arrived from Thebes?

Second Priest. Yes, my lord. They're ready in the mountain.

High Priest. Good. Our gods turn things to their own ends. *(Pauses, moving to center stage.)* This is a dark moment in the history of Egypt. We didn't seek this conflict. But we will win, friends.

(They circle around him. They are all illuminated by the spotlight.)

High Priest. The last word is not said yet. *(Pauses.)* First, we defeat him here in the streets of this city, among the people!

Second Priest. People are powerless.

First Priest. They can do nothing.

Third Priest. They don't count.

High Priest. Wrong! They are powerless and can do nothing, but their doing nothing is a crucial factor. Their doing nothing counts, and we have to make sure they will do nothing!

Second Priest. How?

HIGH PRIEST. As we have done in Thebes and everywhere in Egypt. I want rumors everywhere in the city. In the coming three days, let rumors take-root, sprout, and swiftly ripen before the harvest when we confront him on the crowning day! *(Pauses.)* I want people in a state of paralysis and inaction. Then, we can act! We will make him pay for everything he has done to us!

(Blackout)

Scene Five

(A room in the palace of Akhnaton. Morning. Bek, the master sculptor and architect, is contemplating some images and seems to be unaware of the presence of Toto. A simple melody plays in the distance.)

BEK, *to himself, loudly, while looking at the images.* The beautiful and the truthful … the truthful … the beautiful. How deep and mysterious the relation between the two! *(Moves toward Toto, stops right in front of him, still unaware of his presence.)* The truthful and beautiful …

TOTO, *trying to be decent.* Talking to me, Bek?

BEK, *loudly, still to himself.* Truth and beauty: everything truthful is beautiful. My lord and master, Akhnaton—

TOTO, *interrupting.* He is in the back garden.

BEK, *not paying attention to Toto.* My lord and master, Akhnaton, said that everything truthful is beautiful. *(Turns back to the images of Akhnaton.)* This is indeed truthful. Therefore, it must be beautiful. It is beautiful. *(Becomes aware of Toto's presence.)* How do you like this image, Toto?

TOTO, *unemotionally.* Nice.

BEK. No, no. I'm talking about how it is beautiful because it is truthful. *(Looks at the image.)* This is our lord Akhnaton as he really is. This is new in art—no embellishment, no beautifying—nothing but the truth. As he really is. Everything truthful is beautiful. *(Pauses.)* How would like your image, Toto? As you really are or as you want people to see you? *(Pauses again.)* Truth is beauty?

(Enter Horemoheb. He is very handsome—well-built, moderately tall, and with a strong, trustworthy demeanor. He looks worried and unhappy.)

BEK, *glancing at Horemoheb.* Then comes the question, Is everything beautiful truthful? *(Then, to Horemoheb)* Here comes the man of the sword, general of the Egyptian armies. We're talking, sir, about the relation between beauty and truth. The question is—

HOREMOHEB, *interrupting grimly.* I've no mind for this now, Bek. *(To Toto)* Where is my lord?

TOTO. He's having breakfast with the family in the back garden.

HOREMOHEB. I need to talk to him. This is urgent.

(Voices offstage. Enter Akhnaton, Nefertiti, and Merry, their youngest daughter. Akhnaton'clothes are simple like those in the images. Nefertiti wears a white, flowing dress. She is elegant and beautiful. Her face and movements, however, reveal that her life is dry in some significant way.)

MERRY, *happily following her father, begging.* Please, Dad. Once more.

AKHNATON, *smiling.* Not now.

MERRY. Please, Dad. Just once.

AKHNATON. Just this once. *(Carries her on his shoulders for a few seconds, then returns her to the ground while she screams in happiness.)*

(Merry exits, still shrieking.)

AKHNATON. Good morning, everybody. *(Notices Toto still prostrating himself in sharp contrast to both Bek and Horemoheb, who simply bowed.)* I've told you that we prostrate ourselves like this only to the one and only God.

TOTO, *rising in embarrassment.* I forgot, my lord. I'm awfully sorry my lord. I beg—

AKHNATON, *to Horemoheb, smiling and interrupting Toto.* You're an early bird this morning! But you look worried. *(Pauses.)* There's news for you about Azuro.

HOREMOHEB. I'm here for the same reason, my lord.

AKHNATON. Good. *(Turns to Bek.)* Let's finish with Bek then.

BEK. My lord, everything is almost ready for the festival.

AKHNATON. Almost?

BEK. The entrance to the city, my lord, needs more time.

AKHNATON. Why?

BEK. The fresh consignments of red granite haven't arrived from the Upper Nile yet.

AKHNATON. Why should you waste time on such extravagances, Bek?

BEK. Extravagances? The occasion is great, my lord.

AKHNATON. Still, we need to be simple and moderate. Go ahead with what is available. What else?

BEK, *showing him the image.* We've produced a large number of your image, my lord.

AKHNATON, *looking at the image.* Good. This will make people ready. Good. *(Pauses. Then, to Nefertiti)* Do you like it, dear queen?

NEFERTITI, *not showing much enthusiasm.* I do, my lord.

BEK. Other pictures of my lord and the queen, my lord and the family, my lord and—

AKHNATON, *smiling, patting him on the shoulder.* Enough about me and my family. I want you and all the artists go out for yourselves into the fields and down by the river and do the same. Let everything be true and natural.

BEK. We will do that, my lord.

(Bek bows and exits.)

NEFERTITI, *to Horemoheb, trying to break the tension.* How is my sister, Zemat? I've seen her only once since you arrived from Thebes!

HOREMOHEB. She is fine, ma'am.

AKHNATON, *to Horemoheb after a pause.* A messenger from Tunip has arrived. *(To Toto)* Send for him.

HOREMOHEB, *approaching Akhnaton, carefully.* We shouldn't trust Azuro, my lord. *(Hesitates.)*

AKHNATON, *encouraging.* So … ?

HOREMOHEB. We should send troops to Syria immediately.

(Enter the Messenger. He looks tired, dusty, and travel-stained.)

AKHNATON. Let us hear our friend from Tunip.

MESSENGER, *kneeling in reverence.* My lord, the great pharaoh of Egypt. *(Pauses to open a letter.)* This is from the ruler of Tunip to our lord the great king of Egypt. *(Reading)* From the inhabitants of Tunip, thy servants, may it be well with thee, and at the feet of our lord we fall. My lord, the city of Niy has fallen. If your soldiers and chariots come too late, Azuro will make us like the city of Niy. Now Tunip—thy city, my lord—weeps, and her tears are flowing, and there is no help for us. For twenty years, we have been sending appeals to our lord, the king of Egypt, but there has not come to us a word—no, not one. *(Gives Akhnaton the letter, rises, steps back.)*

AKHNATON, *holding the letter for Toto, who runs to take it.* Let him rest, Toto. He will have our answer today.

(Toto and the Messenger exit.)

AKHNATON, *to Horemoheb.* What do you say?

HOREMOHEB. I came here without knowing about this messenger, because I'm worried about what's been going on in Syria for many years. This message, my lord, means I am right when I suggest sending troops to Syria immediately.

(Toto returns but quickly retreats and exits when Akhnaton glances at him.)

NEFERTITI, *standing.* I need also go to see your mother the queen. *(She exits.)*

AKHNATON, *standing after pondering for a moment.* The problem has existed for twenty years!

HOREMOHEB. We shouldn't waste more time waiting.

AKHNATON. Did we write to Azuro?

HOREMOHEB. I don't trust him, and we shouldn't waste time writing and waiting for his reply. He is of so base a character, he plays one nation against another to have his own land extended at the expense of each. He seems to be true to you and to the Hittites, but he's false to both of you, and chiefly *(hesitating)* false to you.

AKHNATON, *moving away from him toward center stage, considering.* You want to send troops now?

HOREMOHEB. Yes, my lord. He destroyed Niy. We shall destroy him. An eye for an eye and a tooth for a tooth!

AKHNATON. If we go down the road of violence, Horemoheb, and have an eye for an eye and a tooth for a tooth, the world will end up blind and toothless!

(Silence)

HOREMOHEB. My lord, Azuro is a treacherous man, and all he needs is time, and you're— *(He stops, corrects himself.)* I mean we're giving him time, my lord. He'll war against your lesser tribes in Syria, annexing all to himself. Then he'll turn on us. This will be the beginning of *(hesitates)* the collapse of the Egyptian Empire.

AKHNATON, *calmly but decisively.* The collapse has already started here, dear Horemoheb. You want me to send troops to the frontiers, and the heart is corrupt! *(Pauses.)* I'm talking about priorities here. You don't seem to see the link between what is happening in the frontiers and the corrupt heart! It has all started here! *(Another pause)* People in Thebes and everywhere in Upper and Lower Egypt are discontented and restless. Exploitation, greed, and injustice are everywhere. The priests and their gods are behind all that. My battle is here, Horemoheb. I want to begin right. Thank God, the one and only God, for revealing to me the right path. *(Moves toward center stage, turns to Horemoheb, and continues in a sincere, friendly tone.)* I want to begin with what ails the heart of our empire. In the meantime, we write to Azuro, asking him to rebuild what he has destroyed.

HOREMOHEB, *dumbfounded.* He won't, my lord!

AKHNATON. Give him a chance.

HOREMOHEB. He will think we're afraid.

AKHNATON. No, we are not afraid. We will give him and ourselves a chance to change everything. *(Pauses.)* We should teach people how to love and live in peace together. I know this may seem foreign to them after they have been long oppressed and harried with wars and bloodshed. But Egypt is leading the world now and should be the role model. Peace and love will prevail, my friend!

HOREMOHEB. Love and peace! A hundred years from now, the world will still be blindly striving for these ideals in vain. *(A pause)* I'm afraid, my lord, that these ideals cannot govern an empire, and—

AKHNATON, *interrupting.* No, they can. My God is merciful. He is peace and love. His overflowing love reach down the paths of life from mankind to the beasts of the field and even the little flowers. *(Then, decisively)* We will start right after the crowning. I want you to get ready.

(Horemoheb's silence is dissent.)

HOREMOHEB, *bowing.* Excuse me, my lord. *(He begins to leave.)*

AKHNATON, *before Horemoheb reaches the door.* Horemoheb! *(Horemoheb turns to him.)* I can't force you to believe in the one true God. But I know you love Egypt, and you'll have to choose soon.

(Blackout)

SCENE SIX

(A room in Akhnaton's palace. Enter Toto and Mahu.)

MAHU. We could hardly anchor close to the shore. We're fortunate the queen mother arrived safely. The river is angry!

TOTO. Good for us.

MAHU, *amazed.* Why?

TOTO. Security purposes!

MAHU. I don't understand.

TOTO. That's the one thing I like about you, Mahu. You're honest. Lots of people don't understand and pretend they do. But you don't understand, and you don't pretend you do. Honesty …

MAHU, *satisfied.* Thank you, sir.

TOTO, *getting closer.* I'll tell you what I mean by security purposes. When the river is in flood, people can't get across. This means fewer people attending the crowning festival. Of course, I'd like all Egyptians to see the crowning of their prince, but I'm talking as a security man here. We'll be in perfect control of the situation if we have fewer people. The land is in turmoil right now.

MAHU. Got it. You're right, sir.

(Music and chanting get louder.)

TOTO, *looking upstage toward the source of the music.* Do you like it?

MAHU. Yeah!

TOTO. I mean do you believe in the one and only God?

MAHU, *confused.* Honestly, sir, I find it difficult to believe in a god I can't see. But I love Egypt and the prince—

TOTO, *interrupting.* Of course. We all do. *(Smiling)* I saw the queen mother asking you something when you were leaving the barge.

MAHU. She asked me about the prince.

TOTO. She looks worried.

MAHU. Yes, she does.

TOTO, *after a pause.* Listen carefully, Mahu. You know enemies of Egypt and the prince may make use of this transition time. We should be fully alert to any possible dangers.

MAHU. Yes, sir. *(Pauses.)* Yesterday evening some disguised men scared people!

TOTO. I know. Nothing important—personal disputes. You go now and keep me informed of any movement in the court.

MAHU. But I have to go and see Merora first.

TOTO. What for?

MAHU. My lord wants to see him.

TOTO, *trying to look uninterested.* Why?

MAHU. I don't know. There seems to be a new job for him.

TOTO. What job?

MAHU. I don't know. He's a good man, and lots of people love him. I have to run now. *(He exits.)*

TOTO, *to himself.* A new job for Merora? Maybe prime minister? Or high priest of the new religion? *(Pauses.)* But why did he ask Mahu and not me to go to Merora? Maybe Merora's new job is chief of security, my job? No, no, it can't be. I've given my life to serving Egypt, and this idle, low-born Merora comes over and— *(Stops, unable to accept the idea.)* No, no! *(More eagerly, crying)* But why did he ask Mahu and not me to go? Why?

(Blackout)

Scene Seven

(A hall in Akhnaton's palace. Enter Queen Tye and Nefertiti. Tye sinks onto the couch, her head between her hands.)

NEFERTITI. Let me show you the rest of the palace, Queen Mother. *(Notices Tye completely absorbed in her thoughts and fears.)* Queen Mother—

TYE, *turning to her sharply.* Don't you see what's going on? Your husband is risking Egypt for a dream, and you're doing nothing! *(Pauses.)* What kind of wife are you to my son?

NEFERTITI. A loyal wife.

TYE, *shocked to see the blank expression on her face.* A loyal wife! What's wrong, Nefertiti?

NEFERTITI. Nothing.

TYE. Nothing! Surely you're not Nefertiti. Where's the beautiful and ambitious Nefertiti I picked from many for the crown prince? *(A pause)* Another woman?

NEFERTITI. No.

TYE. The harem? Does he visit them?

NEFERTITI. Never.

TYE. Is it because you're sonless?

NEFERTITI, *turning her face away.* I don't know, Queen Mother. I really don't know. I feel there's something blocking the way to his heart.

TYE. Since when?

NEFERTITI. Since we married!

TYE, *shocked.* Are you crazy? You've been married for years and have children!

NEFERTITI. Maybe I'm the reason.

TYE. Why?

NEFERTITI. I came from a common family, and I don't know ...

TYE, *sharply.* Nonsense! I came from a common family too! *(Pauses.)* You're telling me he keeps you away from everything?

NEFERTITI. No, Queen Mother. I don't know how to say it. *(Trying)* He's so gentle. He's a wonderful father and husband, but ... *(Hesitates, stops.)*

TYE. But what?

NEFERTITI. There's always this forbidden area in his heart I'm not allowed to reach.

TYE, *looking into her eyes.* You don't know what he's going to declare on the crowning festival after a couple of days?

NEFERTITI. I know, just like everybody in the court.

TYE. No, Nefertiti. You're not like everybody. *(She tries to stand up, and Nefertiti runs and takes her hand to help her.)* You're still a child. You have to prove to him and to you that you're not like everybody. You have to share everything with him. Try to be always there, ready to help when he needs it.

NEFERTITI. He never asks.

TYE. He doesn't have to express it. Where's your intelligence, Nefertiti? *(Pauses.)* Your husband is alone in a crisis, and you're acting like a child. Where's Horemoheb? Where does he stand?

NEFERTITI. I don't understand!

TYE. What does he think of what my son will do?

NEFERTITI. I don't know.

TYE, *dumbfounded.* You don't know! Your sister, Zemat, is his wife, and you don't know! How often do you see her?

NEFERTITI. I've seen her only once since they've come from Thebes.

TYE. Only once! *(She pauses, pondering.)* Something is stirring! Listen, Nefertiti. You don't know reality. But I, Tye, queen of the great Amenhoteb III, haven't always lived in palaces where one hears only courteous words and flattering phrases. One should never be deceived. *(After a pause) You have an urgent job, Nefertiti.*

NEFERTITI. What job, Mother?

TYE. I need to know the inside of Horemoheb's head. Go see your sister. Use your mind with her and find a way to know what her husband really thinks. Your husband has it in mind to face the priests and destroy their temples, and we should know where the general stands.

NEFERTITI. I'll do anything for my husband, Queen Mother.

TYE. I know, Nefertiti. Hurry up now.

NEFERTITI. Now?

TYE. Yes, now. I smell trouble. *(Nefertiti leaves, and Tye continues to herself.)* Riptah, the high priest. Riptah ... the same old game ...

(Blackout)

SCENE EIGHT

(A room in Horemoheb's house. His wife, Zemat, is lying on a couch listening to the Tara sisters, who are two very old sorceresses. Obviously drunk, she is carelessly listening to what the Tara sisters do and say. The Tara sisters move in a circle while slowly beating drums. Then, they stop and sit on the floor in front of Zemat. The Tara sisters open irregularly shaped bottles of sand and pour out the sand on the floor. They squat over it, rocking to and fro on their heels and uttering mechanical grunts till they appear to go into a kind of trance.)

TARA 1. I see—I see here the sand rises.

TARA 2. But first it is low.

TARA 1. Not for long.

TARA 2. Greatness coming.

TARA 1. I see the double serpent.

TARA 2. I see the crown of Egypt.

TARA 1. On your head.

TARA 2. And on his head.

ZEMAT. Liars! For years you've been promising lies—nothing but lies.

TARA 1, *screaming without looking at Zemat.* No, the sand never lies.

(A pause)

TARA 2, *looking fiercely at the sand.* Signs and lines.

TARA 1. I see ruins.

36

TARA 2. A city burning.

TARA 1. Ashes. Ashes.

TARA 2. And the crown moving … coming … coming …

ZEMAT, *laughing.* Coming to me and Horemoheb? What shall we do?

TARA 1. Nothing!

ZEMAT, *bewildered.* Nothing! *(Sarcastically)* We get nothing if we do nothing!

TARA 2. Wrong! Nothing has never been nothing.

ZEMAT, *impatiently.* Don't speak riddles, Tara sisters!

TARA 1. Come over here to cross the lines and signs.

TARA 2. Seven times.

(Zemat stands up with the cup in her hand, walks downstage unsteadily, and starts crossing the sand while the Tara sisters count. Enter Nefertiti. Shocked to see what is happening, she stops, looking at Zemat and the Tara sisters.)

NEFERTITI. What's this you're doing, Zemat?

ZEMAT, *getting back to the couch, laughing.* Nothing. *(To the Tara sisters)* Tell the queen of Egypt we're doing nothing.

NEFERTITI, *to the Tara sisters.* You two—get out of here.

(They exit.)

ZEMAT, *to herself, loudly.* Nefertiti, my sister, the queen of Egypt, is here—what honor!

NEFERTITI. You still believe these illusions, Zemat?

ZEMAT. You don't like illusions. Why? You believed them once. Do you remember the old man's prophecy that the two of us would be queens of Egypt. We were two little sisters, and—

NEFERTITI, *interrupting.* Zemat …

ZEMAT. And you are now the queen of Egypt, so you don't like illusions anymore. *(Laughs sarcastically.)* You've always been the queen of reality!

NEFERTITI. *You're drunk.*

ZEMAT. You never liked illusions—yeah, the queen of reality. *(Laughing)* That's the one thing I envy you for. *(She drinks.)* You know when and how to sell yourself.

NEFERTITI, *taking the cup from her.* Stop it. You're blind drunk.

ZEMAT. You were the first to declare your faith in the new God. I didn't understand. When I heard you ask our father to go and tell the prince you believed in his God and renounced all other gods, I didn't understand. But I did on the Sed festival when I saw you dance and expose your beauty to get the attention of all, especially *(hesitating)* Horemoheb.

NEFERTITI, *angrily.* Shut your mouth!

ZEMAT, *delirious.* I saw you looking at him. You didn't sleep that night, talking and dreaming. I still remember—

NEFERTITI. You're insane!

ZEMAT, *moving unsteadily away from her.* The next day, Queen Tye chose you for her hideous sick son. You took him and forgot the man of your dreams—my husband—because you're the queen of reality. You—

NEFERTITI, *interrupting, screaming.* Stop it! Stop it! *(Pauses.)* You're out of your mind!

(Silence)

ZEMAT. I'm drunk. I'm only teasing you. *(She laughs convulsively.)* We used to say worse before you married the prince and I married Horemoheb.

NEFERTITI, *interrupting quickly.* I'm here because I haven't seen you for a long time.

ZEMAT, *murmuring.* I'm honored, Nefertiti. I was just teasing you. We used to say far more than this when we were two little sisters.

NEFERTITI. Things are different now.

ZEMAT. True. Things are different. You're the queen now.

NEFERTITI, *after a pause.* What's wrong with you, Zemat? I thought you'd be happy to see me.

ZEMAT. I am. *(She drinks again.)* I really am.

NEFERTITI. You're my sister. I'll always be there when you need me. I expect the same from you. *(Silence)* Of course you'll attend the crowning festival. We'll go together.

ZEMAT. Yes.

NEFERTITI. There's some unrest, but our God will not forsake us.

ZEMAT, *taking another drink.* Yes. There's unrest. There are rumors everywhere. Amun and the other gods are venting their anger at last.

NEFERTITI. You sound like those malicious priests.

ZEMAT, *laughing hysterically.* I'm not stupid, Nefertiti!

NEFERTITI. What do you mean?

ZEMAT. You want me think you're loyal to the new God? I know you!

NEFERTITI. Yes, I am loyal.

ZEMAT. You're loyal only to your insatiable ambition (laughing) and you know it.

NEFERTITI, *rising to her feet in anger.* I am loyal and sincere.

ZEMAT. Talk about anything, but not sincerity. You're incapable of being sincere—this is your most virulent flaw, dear sister.

NEFERTITI. You cannot conceal your envy.

ZEMAT. No ... it isn't envy. I'm only honest. I hate lies. You cannot be sincere. For your ambition, you can do anything. You can change Gods. You can lie even to yourself and tell yourself you love your hideous, sick husband. Your life is a big lie. Would you dare to tell yourself—or your husband—you want him for the throne? *(She paueses.)* Would you dare tell him Horemoheb was—and may be still—the man of your dreams?

(Nefertiti, stunned, moves toward her and fiercely holds her by her arms.)

NEFERTITI. Will you never change? The same vicious, evil ... *(She trails off and turns toward the door. Her eyes show a rude awakening, but she tries to look steady while leaving.)* I never imagined you had such envy and hatred for me!

(End of Act One)

Act Two

Scene One

(Late night. A street in the slums of a village on the other side of the Nile. Akhnaton is in his ordinary clothes, listening attentively to some screaming coming from an isolated old house. Bek does not feel comfortable, though he does not show it.)

BEK. My lord, I ... I don't see—I mean I don't see the point of ... *(He hesitates, looking around.)* We take the boat to the slums of a village on the other side of the Nile at this late hour, and—

AKHNATON, *interrupting,* Hush. You heard that?

BEK. What?

AKHNATON. That.

BEK. What, my lord?

AKHNATON. Somebody is crying.

BEK, *offhandedly.* Children cry before they sleep.

AKHNATON. Not like that!

BEK, *confused.* I don't understand. They cry because they are children, and they are children because they cry. I mean, it's normal, my—

AKHNATON, *moving toward the house.* No! *(He knocks at the door. A feeble Old Woman appears.)* What's the matter, mother?

OLD WOMAN. Nothing.

AKHNATON. Your children are crying.

OLD WOMAN. They're hungry.

AKHNATON. Hungry? Why don't you feed them

OLD WOMAN, *after a pause.* We've no food.

AKHNATON, *stunned, stepping inside.* You've no food! *(Looks around and sees two little girls in shabby, dirty, torn clothes crying beside a clay pot on a fire.)* You're cooking? *(Uncovering the pot)* What's this you're cooking?

OLD WOMAN, *helplessly.* Stones!

AKHNATON, *more stunned.* Stones?

OLD WOMAN. Till they fall asleep. *(Trying to control her tears)* I've nothing to cook for them.

(Akhnaton looks at the clay pot and the two girls and then rushes out and disappears, followed by Bek. Amazed and sad, the Old Woman moves toward the two girls, whose crying becomes louder. Trying to soothe them, she covers them.)

OLD WOMAN. Please, please don't cry. Please.

(Their cries mysteriously respond to the old woman's helplessness and gradually become low, weak, sad, and whimpering—a sad melody telling of loneliness. Enter Akhnaton carrying sacks of grain and food, almost running toward the house, still followed by Bek.)

BEK. Let me carry these things, my lord.

AKHNATON. No. He will ask me, not you, about them.

BEK. Who will ask you, my lord?

AKHNATON. God. He will ask me about the poor and helpless. *(They enter the house.)* They're my lot. *(Putting down the food, he turns to the Old Woman, trying to smile.)* This is for you and the children. *(Pauses.)* They're your children?

OLD WOMAN. My son's.

AKHNATON. Where is your son?

OLD WOMAN. He died in the war. His wife left home and left the kids for me to care for.

AKHNATON. Do you want anything, mother?

OLD WOMAN, *hesitating.* Yes, son.

AKHNATON. What?

OLD WOMAN. I wish our king would be like you!

(Akhnaton turns and leaves. Outside the house, he stands for a moment in contemplation.)

AKHNATON, *to Bek.* What about the rest?

(Bek is bewildered and doesn't know what to say.)

AKHNATON. There are many like this woman, and my God will ask me about them. There are thousands—yes, so many! This is Egypt, except for some corrupt individuals. Egyptians are starving to death. And he was waging wars and building his pyramid and his huge, fake statues! *(Turning to Bek sharply)* Where is your art from this reality, Bek? You've been wasting your talent helping them fake another reality! Why? Why?

(Blackout)

Scene Two

(Akhnaton's palace. The same hall. Enter Tye and Nefertiti.)

Tye, *impatiently.* This is no time for vague answers.

Nefertiti, *confused, the look of rude awakening still in her eyes.* I don't know. *(Almost to herself)* Zemat has been always like that.

Tye. I am not talking about Zemat. I'm talking about her husband, Horemoheb. Whose side is he on?

Nefertiti. The prince's side, of course.

Tye. How did you get this? I mean how did she say it? Or did you hear it from Horemoheb himself?

Nefertiti. He wasn't there. *(Pondering)* Zemat ... Zemat's words. Queen mother, do you ... *(She hesitates, drawing nearer to Tye.)* Do you believe your son? I mean, do you believe in the one and only God?

Tye, *without looking at her, moving toward the couch.* I'm old and tired. My time is short.

Nefertiti, *pleading.* Do you believe in the sole creator, Queen Mother?

Tye, *sitting.* Yes. I do.

Nefertiti. But you never told your son!

Tye. You and my son are still children. You know little about the ways of the world. I hate these cunning priests who seem our friends but are our enemies. Their power and wealth have multiplied over the centuries, and their high priest has become a second pharaoh. I dread the priestly power—a soaring palm whose seemingly holy

44

branches rise toward heaven, while secretly the insidious, hidden roots rule the state. But we have had to live with that. For thirty-seven years, we had to stoop to using guile with those priests. I want you and my son to be guided by our wisdom, which has been bitter in the learning but has not failed us. *(She pauses.)* Open defiance is disastrous.

NEFERTITI. But wouldn't you be supporting your son if he only knew that you also believe in the one and only God? *(Realizing how painful her conclusion is)* He's almost alone.

TYE. No. This isn't the support he needs. He needs to know that pharaohs have been made and unmade by the priests. *(Pauses.)* And you have to help him realize this!

NEFERTITI, *beginning to define herself.* I don't think I can, Queen Mother.

TYE, *standing.* You can, daughter. *(She moves toward Nefertiti.)* Try to lead his thoughts away from the one God.

NEFERTITI. This is the truth he is living. Nobody can change his mind.

TYE. Would you see your husband destroy himself?

NEFERTITI. No, no.

TYE. Then do all you can to protect the throne and your husband, Nefertiti. You're the queen now. I've fought for long years to protect the throne and my husband. But I'm old and tired now. *(Turning to leave)* I need some rest. *(She exits.)*

NEFERTITI, *desperately, to herself.* I cannot be like you, Mother. I can do nothing. He's alone facing the world, and I cannot help him. *(Pauses.)* My sister envies me. Maybe I am not sincere as she says, and this is the punishment? No, I'm sincere. I believe in your God, Akhnaton. You say God knows what's in our hearts. I am sincere.

(From the pavilion comes a sweet melody accompanying a hymn chanted by a chorus. She listens attentively to the words of the hymn:

Lord of the beautiful, O Beautiful One,
With your love, hearts beat
And birds trill.
You live within me, O Lord.)
(pause)

NEFERTITI, *kneeling.* You live within me, my lord. *(Crying)* You live within me, God. And you know I am sincere. *(Putting her head between her hands)* Help us, Lord.

(Enter Akhnaton.)

AKHNATON, *noticing her.* You're here by yourself, Nefertiti? Where's my mother? *(After a pause, he approaches her.)* What's wrong?

NEFERTITI, *standing, trying to hide her tears.* Nothing.

AKHNATON, *holding her hands and drawing her toward center stage tenderly.* What is it, Nefertiti?

NEFERTITI, *gathering her strength.* I need to tell you something, Akhnaton. It may sound ridiculous after we have been married for years, but *(resolved)* I have to say it.

AKHNATON, *smiling.* I'm listening.

NEFERTITI. I believed in your God before I even saw you.

AKHNATON. You were the first woman to believe—

NEFERTITI, *moving away from him.* Let me tell everything, please. Yes, everything. *(A pause)* One evening, I overheard my father secretly reciting the same beautiful hymn that's coming from the pavilion now. The words infused my soul. I asked my father, your teacher, about you and your God. He talked about your wisdom and maturity and how you never lie. I found myself one day confessing my belief in the one God, the sole creator. Then we were invited to the palace for the Sed festival, where I saw you for the first time.

To me, the crown prince and the royal family were an irresistibly attractive, fabulous story. The story attracted me as a moth is drawn to light *(finishing almost to herself)* and then burned by it.

AKHNATON, *compassionately.* Don't be so hard on yourself, Nefertiti.

NEFERTITI, *unrelentingly.* When I first saw you, I was taken aback. *(Hesitates.)* I mean, I—I thought you would never be the man of my dreams. *(Silence)* After marriage, I prayed that God might speak to me as he spoke to you and make me love you. My mother said many husbands and wives live without love. For years I wondered how I would reply if you ever asked me, "Do you love me, Nefertiti?" And I knew I wouldn't find the courage to lie to you. But ... you never asked me!

AKHNATON. You are the first woman to believe. That is more than enough for me, Nefertiti.

NEFERTITI, *pleading.* I am not talking now about God, Akhnaton. I'm talking about you and me. Yesterday you said you want to begin right, and I want us to begin right here, in our house. Is it too late?

AKHNATON, *after a pause.* Only God can change hearts, Nefertiti.

NEFERTITI. When you went to Thebes for the king's funeral and stayed there for weeks, I missed you wherever I was at every hour of the day. Yes, I missed you. I could not believe you occupied so much of my life. For the first time, I realized that without you, I cannot be happy. I longed for you to return. I—I smelled your clothes in the wardrobe. I longed for you to return so that I could throw myself at your feet and tell you without you asking me how much I love you. *(Throwing her hands around his neck)* I love you, Akhnaton.

AKHNATON. I love you too, Nefertiti. *(After a pause)* Praise be to God— at last your love has come! *(Gently and slowly moving away)* I knew all this, Nefertiti. I knew it all when we met at the Sed festival. I saw your eyes—and your mind! You were divided between choices. And I know myself, Nefertiti. I am not handsome or good-looking like some men—Horemoheb, for example.

NEFERTITI, *coming again to him, her voice trembling in deep emotion.* No, Akhnaton. It is you whom my eyes and heart love. Others don't exist for me, and God knows it. And forgive me, please. I didn't know you'd lived with these dark thoughts all these years. You have never said a word that could hurt my feelings in any way!

AKHNATON. How could I do that to you, Nefertiti, when you are my God's beautiful gift to me?

NEFERTITI, *kneeling, kissing his hand.* I love you and your God, Akhnaton.

AKHNATON, *taking her hands in his and leading her to the center of the stage.* I love you.

(They embrace in deep emotion.)

NEFERTITI. From now on, I want to be close—very close—to you. Like Queen Mother who stood beside her husband, I want to share everything with you.

(Akhnaton smiles and looks up toward the door, where some voices come. Enter Mahu.)

AKHNATON. What is it, Mahu?

MAHU. Merora is here, my lord.

AKHNATON. Let him in. *(To Nefertiti, smiling)* You want to share everything with me? *(Takes her hand, leading her toward a simple couch)* This is the beginning. You sit here beside me. You asked for it!

(Enter Merora, who kneels.)

AKHNATON. Welcome, Merora. Do you know why I sent for you?

MERORA. No, my lord.

AKHNATON, *standing and moving away from the couch.* I need your help.

MERORA. I am my lord's servant.

AKHNATON. I have a job for you here. But let me first tell you good news. The pyramid—we have been wasting our country on it, and it is not yet finished. *(Stops, glances at Nefertiti.)* Well, we're not going to finish it. The workers will go back to their homes and fields. No more pyramids or wars! Now, about your job. Merora, you are a God-fearing family man and honest. I want to fix things here in the court and the relationship between the court and the people. *(Looks at Nefertiti, who smiles approvingly.)* You will be the head of the court.

MERORA. I serve my lord anywhere. *(Carefully)* I understand, my lord, that I'll work with Mahu, chief of the guards, and Toto, chief of security here.

AKHNATON. Listen carefully, Merora. You will be responsible for everything in the court. I want exact, honest reports about everything. I don't want lies about people. I want every honest opinion to reach me. I want every Egyptian to feel that he counts in every decision the court makes.

MERORA, *kneeling.* I pray that God helps me that I may be up to the expectations of my lord.

AKHNATON. Be ready then. Say no word about this till you start right after the crowning.

(Merora kneels again and leaves.)

NEFERTITI. I am afraid, Akhnaton.

AKHNATON. Why?

NEFERTITI. The priests of Amon and the other gods—

AKHNATON, *calmly.* Our God is the one and only God. He will not forsake us.

NEFERTITI. I mean we can delay announcing the new religion till after the crowning. I heard that a prince does not become a pharaoh if he is not crowned by the priests of Amon and the other gods.

AKHNATON. I don't need them. I shall be crowned in the open under the sunlight with the blessings of the sole creator and the simple people.

(He holds her hands and leads her to the center of the stage. The sweet hymn melody is heard from afar. The stage is dark, but they are under the spotlight. Their faces show genuine happiness. She is captivated by the magic and sincerity in his words. He is charmed by the expression of deep concern and love on her beautiful face.)

AKHNATON. I love your face. It is so beautiful. *(A pause) Don't be afraid, Nefertiti. I know the change will be a drastic one. But it's God's command. And the people of Egypt deserve it. They have been enslaved for hundreds of years by those priests and their gods. The priests made pharaohs mortal gods to serve their own ends. They have become themselves pharaohs, and Egypt now is nothing but gods and their slaves. (Decisively) Someone should stand up and say no. I am going to be that someone. God has chosen me! (Almost crying)* There are no gods on earth, Nefertiti! I will start with myself. I will be the last pharaoh. I will live like all Egyptians. I will eat, drink, and dress like them. This is what God wants me to do, because there is no god but the one and only God! *(A pause)* Now, to work. We have a lot of work to do after the crowning. *(He moves toward the door.)* We'll rebuild everything. There will be no injustice, no corruption. Egyptians will have the life they deserve! I have seen them suffer while the court celebrates its lies.

NEFERTITI. Strange!

AKHNATON. What?

NEFERTITI. You never liked the court in Thebes! You were always alone!

AKHNATON. I never felt I belonged to the court! I ...

NEFERTITI, *insistently.* Why?

AKHNATON, *moving away from her.* I don't want to talk about …

NEFERTITI, *following him, more insistently.* Please, Akhnaton. I don't want you to be alone again.

AKHNATON. I'm used to it. I've been always alone! *(Pauses.) Long years ago, my father forced me to go with him and my brother, Thutmose, to hunt hippopotamus. The hippos became enraged and overpowered the hunters, overturning all of us into the Nile. In the confusion, I sank below the waves. I couldn't swim. I was slowly sinking toward the river's floor. I was dying. I cried out, "Help me, God. Give me your hands! Give me your hands!" I heard him say, "I will save you to serve me." Then I found myself on the shore. I learned that father, in the heat of the battle and the froth of violent water, had pierced Thut, his son, with a great jab of his lance, killing both the hippo and the boy. On the long voyage home, I drifted in and out of consciousness.* No one spoke to me, but I will never forget my father's words and the strange look on his face when we arrived at the court!

NEFERTITI. What did he say?

AKHNATON. "You will never know how I hate that you have outlived your brother." That's what he said! The day I lost my brother, I felt I also lost the king and my mother! From that day, I learned how to live alone!

NEFERTITI. Certainly he didn't mean it!

AKHNATON, *as if he didn't hear her, in deep sadness.* On his deathbed, he repeated the same words: "You will never know how I hate that you have outlived your brother!"

(Blackout)

SCENE THREE

(A tent in one of the caves in the mountain near Tel el Amarna, before midnight. The High Priest stands in the middle, deeply absorbed in his thoughts. The Third Priest, Second Priest, and Toto are anxiously waiting for him to speak.)

HIGH PRIEST, *turning to Toto, sarcastically.* So tomorrow he'll be crowned under the sunlight with the blessings of his God and the simple people?

TOTO. Yes, my lord.

HIGH PRIEST. Where?

TOTO. In the space right in front of the temple.

HIGH PRIEST. When?

TOTO. Midday! *(A pause)* Queen Tye and two senior citizens will place the crown on his head!

THIRD PRIEST. Queen Tye is cunning, and people love her. I'm afraid she might damage everything!

HIGH PRIEST, *pacing up and down, to Toto.* And still decided about declaring his new religion.

TOTO. And the annihilation of all other deities!

HIGH PRIEST, *no longer pacing, calmly and with confidence.* And we are ready. There is no sleep tonight. *(Pauses.)* Horemoheb and Mahu should not attend the festival tomorrow! I'll take care of Horemoheb. *(To Toto)* You take care of Queen Tye and Mahu. They should not attend the festival!

TOTO. I'll do that, my lord. *(A pause)* What about Merora?

HIGH PRIEST, *smiling.* Your rival?

TOTO. He sent for him yesterday.

HIGH PRIEST. Why?

TOTO. I don't know! He sent Mahu, not me, to him.

HIGH PRIEST. Did they meet?

TOTO. Yes, they did, but nothing was said after the meeting! Maybe Merora will be the prime minister!

HIGH PRIEST. Or the new chief of security. You say he sent Mahu, not you!

TOTO, *deeply worried.* Maybe!

HIGH PRIEST. I promise you, friend, he will never be this or that. *(To all)* Now listen carefully, friends. Tomorrow we have two choices only. Either we survive this challenge or lose everything and die as cowards. There is no room for any mistake. *(He pauses. Then, to the Third Priest)* Tomorrow, a few minutes before the heretic appears, twenty of our men will be in the first row waiting for your signal. To control the rest of the audience, some of our men should be well distributed among them. *(To Toto)* Three of the guards in the procession will be replaced by three of our men, who should be very close to him throughout the procession. *(To all)* You know the rest!

(Enter the First Priest. He looks upset.)

FIRST PRIEST. The young man has disappeared!

HIGH PRIEST. When?

FIRST PRIEST. Just now. The guard told me!

HIGH PRIEST. We should find him. *(To Toto)* He shouldn't reach the court. *(To all)* We have to find him.

SECOND PRIEST. What shall we do if we find him?

HIGH PRIEST, *after a pause.* Kill him! I said there is no room for mistakes! One mistake means the death of all of us.

(The Second Priest and Third Priest leave hurriedly.)

HIGH PRIEST, *to Toto.* This young man may try to reach the court. You better get there now!

(Toto leaves.)

HIGH PRIEST, *to the Third Priest.* I will go now to see Horemoheb.

THIRD PRIEST. It's midnight now, my lord!

HIGH PRIEST. He's an old friend. I know how to give his humor the true bent.

THIRD PRIEST. Shall I go with you?

HIGH PRIEST. No, you stay here. *(Covering himself completely in his cloak)* Keep an eye on everything. *(Leaving)* No sleep till we are done!

(Blackout)

Scene Four

(Toto alone in the court. He is restlessly pacing up and down. A guard rushes into the room.)

GUARD. We got him, sir.

TOTO. Who?

GUARD. The young man. He was roaming around the court. He wants to see the prince!

TOTO. Did he say anything? I mean, did he say why?

GUARD. No, He insists the prince should hear it himself!

TOTO. Get him here.

(The guard rushes out.)

TOTO, *to himself.* He wants to see the prince!

(Enter the guard, pushing the Young Man toward center stage.)

TOTO, *to the Young Man.* You want to see the prince?

YOUNG MAN. Yes, sir.

TOTO. What for?

YOUNG MAN. A matter of life and death, sir.

TOTO, *moving toward him.* Really? What is it?

YOUNG MAN. The prince should hear it himself.

TOTO, *in a fierce, controlled tone.* Do you know me?

55

YOUNG MAN. No, sir.

TOTO. I'm the chief of security. You know what that means? *(Pauses.)* It means I should be the first to know if there is a life-and-death matter as you say. Do you understand?

YOUNG MAN. Yes, but I'm sorry, sir; I'll disclose it only to the prince.

TOTO, *after a long silence.* You don't understand. Listen carefully, young man. You think we don't know what you know? We know it. Egyptians love the prince, but like any ruler, he has enemies. *(He gets close, looking into the Young Man's eyes.)* And they may be mad and plot against our beloved prince. We know everything.

YOUNG MAN, *confused.* But there is another serious matter, sir.

TOTO, *quickly.* What?

YOUNG MAN, *hesitating, looking at the guard.* I can't ... I mean ...

TOTO, *signaling to the guard to leave.* You can speak now.

YOUNG MAN, *getting very close, almost whispering.* I've heard the plotters say they have their man in the court. They didn't mention his name, but he's very close to the prince, and—

TOTO, *theatrically and violently.* How dare you! You're telling me I'm a fool and know nothing about what's going on here? *(Screaming)* Guards! Guards!

(Two guards rush into the room.)

TOTO, *still to the Young Man.* How dare you say one of my men is a traitor? All my men are loyal to the court and our beloved country. How dare you say that? Your tongue should be punished for that! *(Signaling to the guards)* Cut off his tongue!

(The guards move quickly toward the Young Man, who, terribly shocked, tries to resist, but the guards finally cut off his tongue. The Young Man gives a long scream of pain and fear. End of scene four.)

(Blackout)

Scene Five

(The same room in Horemoheb's house after midnight. Zemat is standing by a window with a cup in her hand. Seated on the couch, Horemoheb looks worried and in a bad mood.)

HOREMOHEB, *sarcastically.* Peace and love? Beauty and truth? Peace … love. *(Loudly, to Zemat)* His grandfather, the great Amonhoteb II, once caught and slew seven rulers of those rebellious dominions in Syria, had six of them on a chariot all the way to Thebes for people to see, and the seventh was hung on a tree in our Nubian land to scare all rebels! That was how the Egyptian Empire was created. That was how Egyptians maintained their huge empire! *(A pause)* Now the prince is talking about nothing but peace and love! I thought he would begin, like his grandfathers, by teaching the rebels in those dominions how to treat us! I told him we should send troops immediately!

ZEMAT, *turning to him sharply.* Wake up, Horemoheb! The prince will never send troops! *(Drinks.)* Wake up!

HOREMOHEB. What do you mean?

ZEMAT. He will never send troops or allow you to lead troops!

HOREMOHEB, *dumbfounded.* Why?

ZEMAT. Horemoheb, my husband, the great warrior, is an innocent child!

HOREMOHEB, *angrily.* Why, woman?

ZEMAT, *after a pause.* Your prince will be crowned tomorrow. He will be the great pharaoh of Egypt. But he knows you sit high in all the people's hearts, and sending troops led by you will make you rise more in their eyes. This is the reason he will never send troops, and he will never tell you this. Instead, he gives us this crap about peace and love!

HOREMOHEB, *standing.* No, no. He is not like that. You don't know Akhnaton.

ZEMAT. I know him. He is weak and malicious. Peace and love are nothing but words he uses to cover up his weakness and envy of you!

HOREMOHEB, *not wanting to believe it, moving toward her.* You don't understand! He has been like that all his life. He has always talked about peace and love. *(He finds it difficult even to say.)* And he does not envy me!

ZEMAT, *persistently.* He does envy you!

HOREMOHEB. No, no. He does not. *(Moves away from her.)* You don't know him!

ZEMAT. Wake up, Horemoheb! Wake up before it is too late!

HOREMOHEB, *stepping toward her again.* You don't understand him. *(Takes the cup from her.)* You drink too much. *(Puts the cup on the table, looks concerned.)* I'm tired. *(Puts off the lights and keeps one candle on, then moves toward the door.)* I need to go to bed.

(There is a knock at the door)

HOREMOHEB, *turning.* What is it, Nye?

(Enter Nye, the maid.)

NYE. Someone wants to see you, sir.

HOREMOHEB. At this late hour? Who is he?

NYE. He does not want to say, sir. He says he is a friend!

HOREMOHEB, *amazed.* A friend! *(To Zemat, after a pause)* Go in now. *(To the maid, loudly)* Let him in.

(Enter the High Priest, who takes off his cloak and stands by the door.)

HOREMOHEB, *surprised, moving toward him*. Our holy father, the high priest! *(Kneels and kisses his hand.)* I thought you were in Thebes!

HIGH PRIEST. I left Thebes a few days ago. I had to. Nobody knows I am here. *(A pause. Then, sarcastically)* You know I am not invited!

HOREMOHEB. I am sorry for that, father. I can do nothing about it! I am not ungrateful. I have not forgotten what you have done for me. You singled me out and took a genuine interest in my career from the beginning. *(Embarrassed)* But believe me—

HIGH PRIEST, *speaking with dignity*. I know, my son, that a noble and courageous heart does not forget benefits received—only a mean nature is embarrassed and seeks to forget. I did not think for a minute you would have forgotten the old days.

HOREMOHEB, *still embarrassed*. No, that is true, father.

HIGH PRIEST. I came secretly in disguise here not to ask a favor *(pausing, moving toward him)* but to thank you.

HOREMOHEB, *even more embarrassed*. Thank me! For what?

HIGH PRIEST. People talk about how you courageously faced the prince, asking him to send troops to help our brothers in Syria. They also speak about your intention not to attend the crowning because you are not happy about what he has done to us and the orders he intends to issue tomorrow.

HOREMOHEB, *confused*. Indeed, I asked him to send troops, but honestly, I know nothing about my intention not to attend the crowning!

HIGH PRIEST. Perhaps this is what the people want you to do. They love you. You have become their hero, and they expect you to do what they cannot do. That is what a hero stands for!

HOREMOHEB, *turning away.* I do not know how to put it, father. *(A pause)* I have never been *(hesitating)* a religious sort of man!

HIGH PRIEST. But you have been a man of loyalty. That's what Egyptians like about you. You have a noble and courageous heart—one that cannot help but be loyal to old friends.*(A pause)* Listen, my son. Our temples have been destroyed. Our treasure has been confiscated. But I am not here to complain, because we are not broken yet, and we will never be broken. I am here, my son, because I am still interested in your career.

HOREMOHEB. I do not understand.

HIGH PRIEST. Your not attending the crowning may be of little significance for the prince. For the people, it means a lot.

HOREMOHEB. Why?

HIGH PRIEST. Because you are their wise and courageous hero. *(He pauses, moves toward him, stops, looks him in the face.)* Becoming chief of armies should not be the crowning achievement of the people's hero. Your not attending the crowning is nothing, but it could be a crucial step in your career! *(Moves toward the door.)* I should go now. *(Stops at the door.)* Remember that I came as an old friend who has been always true to you. *(Disguising himself ing the cloak)* Good night! *(He leaves.)*

HOREMOHEB, *stunned, to himself.* A crucial step in my career!

(Enter Zemat)

HOREMOHEB. Of course you heard everything?

ZEMAT. What will you do?

HOREMOHEB. I don't know.

ZEMAT, *quickly.* Why? It's obvious—don't go to the crowning.

HOREMOHEB. And how would we justify it to—

ZEMAT, *interrupting*. Say I am sick or dying and you could not leave me!

HOREMOHEB, *worried and confused, pacing about*. No, no.

ZEMAT, *going to him*. My beloved Horemoheb, Egypt is in turmoil, and we do not know which side will win. Your not going is nothing, but it will help you strike a balance.

(Horemoheb moves away, stopps with his back to her, pondering.)

HOREMOHEB. Nothing?

ZEMAT, *following him, caressing his shoulders*. Nothing, Horemoheb.

HOREMOHEB. Akhnaton is my friend.

Zemat. Your friend will never allow you to lead troops again. It is all clear, my beloved. But you will remain the hero of the people. They worship you, and you have the army behind you. He is jealous of you, because you are a hero. He wants to put an end to your career. (She kisses his head from behind.) You will save Egypt from what she is facing now. (A pause) You look every inch a king, Horemoheb!

(He turns to her, his face showing a strange expression of worry and contained excitement.)

ZEMAT. Yes, Horemoheb, you look every inch the pharaoh of Egypt!

(Blackout)

Scene Six

(The same hall in Akhnaton's court. The queen mother is seated on the couch. She looks deeply worried. Enter Nefertiti. She is very happy.)

Nefertiti, *noticing her.* Good morning, Mother. We're all dressed. You're late!

Tye. I don't feel well.

Nefertiti, *moving toward her.* Why, Mother?

Tye. I did not sleep well. *(Almost to herself)* Bad dreams!

Nefertiti. My father used to say dreams are our fears and desires.

Tye. That's true. But some are telling visions!

Nefertiti, *after a pause.* Today is the crowning of Akhnaton. We should be happy, Mother.

(Enter Akhnaton. He is happy and confident.)

Akhnaton, *kissing his mother.* Good morning, Mother. Are we all ready? We move shortly.

Tye, *looking at his clothes in amazement.* You will be crowned in these clothes?

Akhnaton, *calmly smiling.* Yes, Queen Mother.

Tye. The people will see their pharaoh for the first time dressed like that?

Akhnaton. Nothing wrong with that, Mother. Let the people see the king of Egypt simply dressed and living a simple life. Let them know that I am only a man like themselves. Let them know the great truth—all men are brothers.

TYE, *sharply*. No, you are not like them. You are the king—the great pharaoh of Egypt. You should be always garmented in awe. Put on ceremonial robes and—

AKHNATON, *still smiling*. That is not my way, Mother.

TYE. I know the people. Their minds are simple, childish. I pray of you, Son, let the people be awed and dazzled by the magnificence of their king. You are a man apart. *(Almost screaming)* You are the great pharaoh!

AKHNATON. A god, not a man—that is what you would say. No, mother. I am no god. There is only one true God…

TYE, *rising, interrupting in anger*. I am tired. *(Moving toward the door)* I need rest.

NEFERTITI, *going after her*. You will attend the crowning, Mother?

TYE, *turning to her in despair*. I don't think I can. *(She leaves.)*

NEFERTITI, *returning, trying to smile*. We should be happy today. *(She notices the sad expression on his face and moves toward him.) The queen mother is tired now, and—*

(Enter Mahu)

MAHU, *kneeling*. General Horemoheb will not be able to attend the festival, my lord.

AKHNATON. Why?

MAHU. His servant says the general's wife is sick. *(He kneels and leaves.)*

NEFERTITI, *to herself*. No, she isn't sick. This is a lie! I know you, Zemat. *(Turns to him and sees he has become more worried.) No, no, Akhnaton. You shouldn't look sad. This is the first day your people see you. (Embraces him.) You should look cheerful*

AKHNATON, *gently moving toward the center of the stage.* Strange!

NEFERTITI. What?

AKHNATON, *after a pause.* I knew!

NEFERTITI, *following him.* Knew what?

AKHNATON. I knew Mother and Horemoheb would not attend the crowning.

NEFERTITI. How?

AKHNATON, *bewildered.* The dream!

NEFERTITI. What dream?

(A melody telling of loneliness, fear, hope, and resurrection is heard from afar.)

AKHNATON. A strange vision I had after the dawn.

NEFERTITI, *worried.* Tell me, Akhnaton.

AKHNATON. It was like a journey ... a long way ... and I wanted Mother and Horemoheb to accompany me. I looked behind me, but I didn't see them. I called out, and they didn't answer me. But I had to keep going. I saw faces I didn't like. It became dark, and I felt trapped! I called my God. Then I saw myself at a crossroads. I didn't know which way to take. I called my God again. I kept calling and calling! *(A pause. Hymns are heard.)* And suddenly, I saw lights and heard sweet hymns coming from one of the roads. *(His face grows full of wonder.)* I walked toward the lights, and I saw the beautiful, smiling faces of three young men welcoming me. They introduced themselves as my sons!

NEFERTITI. Your sons?

AKHNATON. Yes, my sons. *(A pause)* They didn't speak our language, but I understood every word they said. They took me to their followers. They were thousands—millions—all chanting with their faces toward heaven, waiting for him to appear!

NEFERTITI. Who?

AKHNATON, *too absorbed in the dream to hear her.* Then light filled the place. I couldn't look up, because light covered earth and sky. We all disappeared in the light. We became him! And I heard the light chanting his name. I heard him chanting his name …

(The hymns gradually fade away. There is silence.)

NEFERTITI. So it ends well!

AKHNATON, *turning to her.* I heard you calling me and crying!

NEFERTITI, *startled.* In the dream?

AKHNATON. Yes, but I couldn't answer, as if we were in two different worlds! *(A pause. Then, trying to cheer her up)* I was happy when I woke up.

(Enter Toto)

TOTO, *kneeling.* The procession starts now, my lord. The chariot is ready.

AKHNATON. No need for the chariot. We will go on foot. Tell Merora he will accompany us.

TOTO, *kneeling again.* I will, my lord.

(Enter Bek with a covered statue in his hand)

BEK, *to Nefertiti, uncovering the statue, which depicts Nefertiti's face.* My lord and master has designed this for you, ma'am.

NEFERTITI. Oh, so beautiful. *(To Akhnaton)* When did you do this? *(She looks again at the statue, moves toward Akhnaton, and holds his hands in love.)* No, I am not that beautiful!

BEK, *after a pause, to Akhnaton.* There is something I should tell, but …

AKHNATON. What?

BEK. Your images were defaced every place we hung them!

NEFERTITI, *angrily*. Why? Who dares to do that?

TOTO, *calmly kneeling*. I am not sure it was a deliberate act, my lord.

AKHNATON. It could be the priests' followers.

TOTO. I will investigate this. But the city is safe, as you will see, my lord. People are now waiting to see their beloved king.

AKHNATON. Let's move then.

(Blackout)

Scene Seven

(*The space in front of the temple where the audience is waiting for Akhnaton to appear. Drums and music of the procession are heard from afar. The priests and their followers are among the audience, anxiously waiting to see Akhnaton. Upstage left, two men enter and move toward the audience.*)

First Man. The gods are angry.

Second Man. It's the closing of the temples.

First Man. We haven't seen a flood like this. Thunder and lightning did not stop last night! It shows the impatience of our gods. The end of the world is coming!

Second Man, *looking around.* Hush!

First Man, *recklessly.* Things can't get worse. The spirit of the people is broken. It is the curse of the gods. I heard he will declare the new religion now! (*A pause. Then, in a loud voice to make others hear him*) No true pharaoh would desert his father's gods!

(*The people around the two men murmur.*)

First Man, *sarcastically,* The new God has no shape or substance. But he loves us and is never angry or jealous of the old gods. The proof is that the high priest has been murdered by the order of Akhnaton to please the God of love and peace.

(*Shocked and frightened, the people murmur.*)

Third Man, *to his neighbor.* You heard that?

Fourth Man. Hush, spies are everywhere!

(Enter Akhnaton, Nefertiti, Toto, Merora, a guard carrying the crown, and the three guards. Shouts rise, and the three guards discretely move to circle Akhnaton.)

FOURTH MAN, *whispering.* Where is the pharaoh?

THIRD MAN. The one between the guards.

FOURTH MAN, *stunned.* Why is he dressed like that? No, no. You are sure he is the pharaoh?

THIRD MAN. Hush!

AKHNATON, *looking at the faces in the first row and then turning to Nefertiti.* I don't like these faces. I saw them before!

NEFERTITI. Where?

AKHNATON. In the dream!

TOTO, *to Akhnaton.* Shall we start, my lord?

(Akhnaton nods to Merora, who steps forward and turns to face the audience, loudly addressing the people.)

MERORA. Today we celebrate the crowning of our beloved prince. It is a great day in the history of Egypt, a day Egypt and Egyptians deserve, because they have given the world knowledge and wisdom. They have established a civilization leading the world now. Today your beloved Akhnaton will announce significant orders he himself wrote. These orders are a huge step for human civilization, a step which will put an end to injustice and bring about justice, peace, and love, a step which will make all men brothers, not gods and slaves. But it is also a step which will make men slaves only to the one true God.

(A pause; murmuring from the audience is heard.)

MERORA. That is why our beloved prince has chosen to be crowned here by you, his people, with the blessings of the one and only God. *(He nods to the guard carrying the crown.)* We begin first with the crowning. *(Bows to Akhnaton, who steps toward the center of the stage.)*

FIRST MAN, *standing and shouting from the audience.* You are talking about peace and love! Know then that my brother was beaten to death by Akhnaton's men.

AKHNATON, *turning to him, amazed.* No, this cannot have happened!

FIRST MAN, *persistently.* Yes, it happened. He was lashed naked to a pillar by your men. *(Screaming, looking significantly to the other men)* It happened, and my brother is not the only one. There are many others.

OTHER MEN, *standing simultaneously.* Yes, it happened.

TOTO, *calmly,* to Akhnaton. We will investigate this, my lord. *(Loudly to the men)* Give us the names of all those beaten to death. Come forward. Come.

(The three priests and their followers move toward the stage while the three guards tighten the circle around Akhnaton. The priests and their followers are now on the stage.)

MERORA, *stepping forward to meet them.* Back to your places.

(They get closer, screaming.)

MERORA. I said back to your—

(One of the three guards stabs him from behind. Merora falls.)

AKHNATON, *fiercely screaming.* Merora! *(He turns to the guard, but the other two guards violently seize him and force him to go with them.)*

AKHNATON, *severely shocked.* What are you doing? *(Trying in vain to free himself, shouting)* Leave me! Leave me!

NEFERTITI, *shocked, hysterically trying to reach for Akhnaton, pushed back by the guard.* You cannot do this, cowards. Leave him. (Tries again in vain but is cruelly pushed. Seeing Akhnaton taken away, she helplessly falls on her knees, crying.) No, no, you cannot do this to him, cowards. No, No.

SECOND PRIEST, *glancing at the dead body of Merora and the fleeing people, to the Third Priest.* People are fleeing!

HIGH PRIEST. Why? They shouldn't. Tell them they shouldn't panic. *(He moves toward center stage, where he stops and turns to the audience.)* Tell them we are doing this to protect you. We have done this for you, for your security and peace, for thousands of years of civilization and progress. We are doing this for you and your gods—Yes, you and your gods!

(Blackout)

Scene Eight

(The tent in the cave, which occupies upstage right. The stage is dark, but Akhnaton, chained to the pillar of the tent, can be seen downstage right. The Young Man, absolutely shattered and almost unconscious, lies on the floor. Downstage left, the High Priest is pacing about, and the other three priests are very tense while looking at Akhnaton, who looks very tired and shocked. The melody of the dream and the echo of Nefertiti's crying are heard from afar.)

HIGH PRIEST, *stopping, turning his face in the direction of the echo.* What is that?

FIRST PRIEST. Nefertiti is walking the streets looking for him and crying.

SECOND PRIEST, *looking upstage and seeing rising flames and smoke.* The city is on fire!

THIRD PRIEST. We are running out of time, my lord.

(A pause. The High Priest moves upstage toward Akhnaton, stops before him, and bows in a theatrical way.)

HIGH PRIEST. I apologize for not attending your crowning, my lord. I wanted to, but you did not invite me. It was great. I missed it.

AKHNATON, *slowly rising to his feet with great force of will.* You will never get away with this.

HIGH PRIEST, *as if he hasn't heard him.* It was great. But, honestly, I did not like it, because it was unreal, and I like the real thing. We wanted you to be crowned in our temples with the blessings of our gods like your father and grandfathers, the great pharaohs. They were mortal gods. We wanted to make you, like them, a mortal god, but you failed us, my lord. Why? Why?

71

AKHNATON, *crying out.* You are blind. There are no gods but the sole creator—

HIGH PRIEST, *interrupting sharply.* Still dreaming! *(Pauses, moves away downstage, stops, and turns to him.)* There are gods, and there will be always gods. Amon Ra, Seth, Sutekh, Baal, and Ishtar are gods. Your grandfathers, the great pharaohs, were gods. There will be always pharaohs. *(Moving toward him)* You know why? Because people need them. That has been the deal since the beginning of life, and no one can turn back the clock. Gods are the sovereign power that enforces protection for all citizens.

AKHNATON. Citizens? You mean slaves. You create gods to enslave people and justify injustice and corruption. People are born free and have one god, Riptah. People—

HIGH PRIEST, *interrupting sharply.* People? Where are those people you are talking about? What did they do for you? They fled from your city and left you alone. They all fled *(glancing at the Young Man)* except this fool! *(Pauses.)* And where is your one God? Where is he? Why did he forsake you?

AKHNATON. No, He didn't forsake me. I am his messenger, and he will not forsake me. *(His body shivering, he cries out his words as if these words have become his only companions.)* He will never forsake me. I am not alone. I am his prophet and messenger. He will never leave me. I am not alone. I am not alone.

(Hymns are clearly heard, and Akhnaton is now completely living the dream.)

HIGH PRIEST, *moving toward him calmly.* We are now at a crossroads. We have only two ways: your way—and as you see, we have come to the end of it—or our way. Our way is still open. You can still be the great pharaoh of Egypt. We will go to Thebes and crown you there in our temples. We will tell the people that the prince who appeared in this city was not you. *(A pause)* What say you now?

AKHNATON. No, I don't want your lies.

(The High Priest paces again, thinking, stops, and turns and moves toward Akhnaton.)

HIGH PRIEST. Speaking of lies, there was a queen very wise but, unfortunately, barren. She wanted a son for the throne, and we helped her create a lie!

AKHNATON. What are you talking about?

HIGH PRIEST. About lies, about you!

AKHNATON. I'm Akhnaton, the prince ...

HIGH PRIEST. Yes, you're Akhnaton and the prince *(Getting close, looking into his eyes)* but not our great Amonhotep's son.

AKHNATON, *trying to hold though his soul is collapsing.* Damn corrupt liar!

HIGH PRIEST. No, I'm not. Queen Tye knows. *(Seeing the effect of his words on Akhnaton's shocked face)* I'm not a liar. Give yourself time and consider what I'm offering you. I'm offering you a lot, and you've got nothing ... nothing ... nothing, my lord! The dream is gone. Wake up, my lord! *(Retreats downstage to where the three priests are anxiously waiting.)*

THIRD PRIEST, *to High Priest, whispering impatiently.* We've no choice, my lord! If we let him live, we die and lose everything!

SECOND PRIEST. Yes, we have no choice, my lord!

HIGH PRIEST, *with a confident smile, looking at Akhnaton.* Give him time. He'll come to our way. *(Leaving, followed by the two priests)* Things will be different in the morning!

(Silence)

(Groaning with pain, the Young Man slips in and out of consciousness.)

AKHNATON, *still shocked, his mind racing with memories, to himself.* Queen Mother! No, she is not my mother, and he—he is not my father! *(Pauses.)* Who am I? Who am I? A dream? Yes, a dream! And nothing left of the dream but humiliation! Humiliation! No, no, no! *(Crying out)* Are you there, God? *(Silence)* I'm alone, defeated, nothing left but humiliation! I'm alone, God! Alone. Are you there, God? You are there! Help me! Give me your hands! Give me your hands! Perhaps I am not their son, but my dream is legitimate. My dream is legitimate, God, and you know it!

(Silence. The Young Man groans. He is now fully conscious.)

AKHNATON, *turning to him.* I am sorry, son!

(Startled and confused, the Young Man stands, taking a dagger out of his clothes.)

AKHNATON. I am sorry! I didn't mean it. I didn't know the dream would come to this! I didn't want to build pyramids for me, but I wanted every Egyptian to be himself a pyramid! I wanted to free Egyptians from themselves. I wanted them to believe in one God, because they will never fear or enslave one another if they fear and believe in one God! But they don't know! They don't know, and it does not need a prophet to know! I am sorry, friend!

(The Young Man moves toward Akhnaton, kneels, and kisses Akhnaton's hands, crying.)

AKHNATON, *after a pause.* Don't cry, friend. My sons are coming. All prophets after me are my sons. I see them coming! *(Turning his face in the direction of light, music, and hymns coming from offstage)* My sons are here now with me! O my God, I am not alone. I am not alone! *(Exalted and pacified)* I am ready now, my God! Yes, I am ready!

(Silence. By gesture, the Young Man shows he will defend Akhnaton using the dagger.)

AKHNATON. You want to defend me?

(The Young Man nods.)

AKHNATON, *gathering his strength.* Yes ... you can defend me. Your dagger will save the dream from humiliation!

(The Young Man runs to the corner, burying his head in his hands and signifying his rejection of the idea.)

AKHNATON. Do you believe?

(The Young Man nods.)

AKHNATON. Believers fear no death! They fear nothing! They never get intimidated or allow their dream to be humiliated! You hear me?

(The Young Man frantically shakes his head, refusing again.)

AKHNATON, *after a pause.* Listen to me, this is no mercy killing. We are not cowards. We are believers, and this is our way to keep the dream alive! Martyrs and believers have one way to keep the dream alive! *(A pause)* Come on! We've gone a long way for our dream. What's left is nothing but humiliation. *(Another pause)* Believers keep the dream brave and free! And you are a believer! You fear nothing! Come on! Come on! You will keep the dream alive. We will keep it brave and free! Yes! Yes! Brave and free!

(Dagger in his hand, the Young Man slowly rises and moves toward Akhnaton ...)

(The Curtain falls)

Winter Dreams:
A Play in Two Acts

CHARACTERS

Kate

Martin — Her son

Jackie — Kate's friend

Professor Rex

The Minister

Mr. Edward — School principal

Tim — TV reporter

A Man

A Crowd of People

Old Man

Old Woman

Time: — The Present

Place: — An Unidentified Small American Town

ACT ONE

(An Old Man with a liquor bottle in his hand and an Old Woman are sitting on a park bench. There is a plastic bag beside her on the bench. Behind them and upstage, there is a tree with no leaves. In the back corners of the stage appears a house across from a beautifully decorated church. The vacant area between the house and the church has the shape of a missing apex, behind which higher peaks covered with snow can be glimpsed.)

OLD WOMAN, *abruptly, resolutely.* Surely, this is the day of atonement. *(A slight pause)* A boy leaving his school and preaching on the streets!

(The Old Man does not respond.)

OLD WOMAN. They say television reporters are here. Kids are imitating him and stirring up a riot in the whole town!

(The Old Man drinks but still does not respond.)

OLD WOMAN, *after a pause.* You heard him preaching? I heard him twice. *(Sadly)* He broke my heart. I feel he is anointed. *(With determination)* Yes, he is anointed. *(A long pause)* The boy has been through a lot. *(After a pause, turning to him)* Have you seen him? Have you seen Martin? He has the face of an angel. His eyes are so beautiful. He is just wonderful. But he has suffered enough. *(Indignantly glancing at the house)* She is a disgrace. *(A pause.)* A shame.

(The Old Man looks at her but does not speak. He drinks.)

OLD WOMAN, *looking at him.* Why don't you talk? *(Angry)* I'm talking to you. What is the matter with you?

(He drinks.)

OLD WOMAN. Stop drinking! You're already blind drunk. *(Suspicious)* Who are you?

OLD MAN, *looking closely at the label on the bottle in his hand.* A fine name for wine. *(Reading)* Thunderbird. *(A slight pause)* A fine name!

OLD WOMAN, *looking at the bottle.* Cheap.

OLD MAN. Yeah, cheap. But it gets me high. When I'm not drinking, there's very little I can do.

OLD WOMAN, *scared.* Who are you?

OLD MAN, *after a pause.* You know I'm not an avoider. I'm not a coward. But life is. *(A pause)* Yeah. Life is.

OLD WOMAN, *getting up, reaching for her plastic bag.* Who are you?

OLD MAN, *glancing at the bag.* What's in this bag?

OLD WOMAN. It's Nefr's dinner.

OLD MAN. What?

OLD WOMAN. My cat's food. I have to feed her and her babies before I go to bed.

OLD MAN. Where is she?

OLD WOMAN, *gesturing at the wooden box on the church's fence.* There.

OLD MAN, *crudely.* Crazy old fool.

OLD WOMAN. Who?

OLD MAN. You. *(She moves toward the wooden box.)* You know why? Because you're out here in this mean weather to feed a cat and nobody cares about you. *(A pause)* Let her die, you old fool.

OLD WOMAN, *pulling herself together and stopping beside the box, loudly.* You dumb barbarian! Do you know she sometimes cries emotional tears? *(Opening the bag)* Dumb inhuman.

OLD MAN, *incredulously.* Emotional tears! Crazy old fool.

(The Minister appears. He seems to be waiting for someone. He looks around and notices the Old Man drinking.)

MINISTER, *moving toward him.* You cannot do this here, man. Don't you believe in God?

OLD MAN. Sure I do. I have proof.

MINISTER. What?

OLD MAN, *coldly.* I've never stepped into your church.

MINISTER, *looking closely into the Old Man's face, realizing he is drunk.* Profound, indeed. *(He moves two steps away.)* Great!

(Edward, the school principal, enters hastily from the right. He is in evident disquietude.)

EDWARD. I don't know, father, what the hell is going on in this damn town. People are blaming my school for the riot Martin has stirred while they all know we're not the problem. *(Agitated)* We are not the problem. *(More agitated, almost shouting)* My school is perfect. The teachers are fully dedicated, and—

OLD MAN, *loudly, to the Old Woman.* Crazy fool.

EDWARD, *shocked, embarrassed.* What's that?

MINISTER. Nothing. Let's move down there.

(They move downstage.)

EDWARD, *furiously.* And those damn reporters—

MINISTER, *interrupting.* Calm down, Mr. Principal, please.

EDWARD, *almost simultaneously, in real fury.* I won't talk to any of them. They all tell the same damn lies. *(With determination)* No! I won't talk to any of them. I tossed one of them out of the school today!

MINISTER. I guess he's the one who called a few minutes ago. I don't mind talking to him. I'm expecting him now.

EDWARD, *still furious.* You can do whatever you like, father, but I'll never talk to any of those damn liars.

MINISTER. Relax, Edward, please. I'm telling you I can handle him.

EDWARD, *after a pause.* Father, I'm here for something else.

MINISTER. What?

EDWARD, *suddenly pleading.* Somebody has got to talk to Martin's mother, Kate. The kid is in a crisis. That woman never attends any of our PTA meetings. She doesn't even bother to respond to the school's letters. *(Getting furious again)* And they're blaming the school! Those damn women do nothing but spread their legs, get those kids, and send them to us— *(He stops, feeling embarrassed.)* I'm sorry, father. Excuse my language. The whole thing drives me crazy! *(After a pause, looking at him)* That's why, father, I don't want to talk to those damn reporters. They take a slip of the tongue like this, and the next day you'll read the headline in their papers *(loudly)* "Principal Says Women Spread their Legs!" *(Pleading, fixing his glasses)* Please, father, talk to his mother. It's time for straight talk.

OLD MAN, *ironically, to the Old Woman.* Emotional tears! Crazy old fool.

OLD WOMAN, *angrily.* Shut up. Shut up. *(Feeding the cat)* Dumb, inhuman man.

MINISTER, *reflectively.* Well, I did intend to talk to her, but after what she did …

EDWARD. What?

MINISTER, *bitterly*. It's really funny. *(A pause)* She wrote a petition and had it signed by some people here. Then she sent the petition to the governor, who sent me a copy.

EDWARD. What petition, father?

MINISTER. She wants to change this church into a theater.

EDWARD, *stunned*. A theater! This church! *(Looking at the house)* That woman is really strange. *(Looking for the word)* Imbalanced!

MINISTER. As you know, she's an actress. *(A pause)* She has had all her performances cancelled in every place she went to.

EDWARD. Yeah, I heard about that.

MINISTER. Even the single play she wrote was cancelled before opening in New York last month for the strange things in it. Now she's turning to our church.

EDWARD. I heard all that about her and her views. Honestly, I can't understand why she's doing all that!

MINISTER, *calmly*. I am trying. *(After a pause, staring at the church)* Thirty years ago, this church was a theater that used to produce cheap things because, you know, our town originally was a place of tradesmen, fishermen, and occasional summer visitors. Thank God we managed to install this beautiful church in the old building. Now—

EDWARD, *interrupting*. Forgive me, father, for interrupting you, but I have to go before that damn reporter comes. *(Quickly)* And please talk to her!

MINISTER. Actually, I called her today, but Professor Rex—you know him?

EDWARD. Yeah, that funny guy living with her who dresses like a woman.

MINISTER. He said she wouldn't speak to anyone. *(A slight pause)* Before you go, I want to know how Martin is doing in school. His grades, I mean.

(Martin appears at the far end of the empty apex between the house and the church. He is carrying the Bible and looks distressed and agonized. He is noticed only by the Old Woman, who looks at him in sympathy and sorrow.)

EDWARD, *in a hurry.* He is doing wonderfully despite the emotional stress. In fact, he is excellent though abnormally shy and quiet. Nothing particular about him except that he has a unique ability to relate whatever happens in school to the Bible. His teachers and I wonder how he does it! I tried to do it once, and I didn't understand a word! I don't know how he does it. I better run before that damn reporter comes.

(He hurries to the right, but the TV reporter and a cameraman followed by a crowd of people stop him.)

REPORTER, *smiling.* I'm glad to see you again, Mr. Principal. I hope you've changed your mind and—

EDWARD, *shouting while covering his face with his hand.* No, I have not and will not!

(He flees the stage.)

REPORTER, *following the principal with his eyes.* A funny guy! *(Turning to the Minister with a smile)* Thank you, Mr. Minister, for being willing to talk to our channel news live at six. *(Gesturing to the cameraman to zoom up on the Minister)* Mr. Minister.

OFFSTAGE VOICE. Tim, you're on the air. Go ahead.

REPORTER. Thank you, Steve. *(Turning to the Minister)* Mr. Minister, any comments? Some say it is a mockery of the church!

MINISTER, *quiet, assured.* No, I do not think so.

REPORTER. Is it a school problem?

MINISTER. It's not that, either.

REPORTER. A home problem?

MINISTER, *cautiously.* Well, we can't discuss this on the air, but let me put it this way: the older patterns of domestic life have reached a point of crisis, and it will be a long time before the Christian response to the new situation becomes clear.

REPORTER. I don't understand!

MINISTER. Well, *(a slight pause)* in our modern age, people believe that self-fulfillment is the paramount aim of life, and given its understanding of freedom, modern life tries to liberate itself from the belief in God. Our objective—I mean the church's objective— is to keep reminding people that God is not the symbol of power over man but rather the symbol of power in and through man; that is, the symbol of the release of man's power and its orientation toward growth and liberation.

(A man jumps from the crowd and stands in front of the camera.)

MAN, *shouting in the microphone.* If your hair is dead, it is dead. But if it is asleep, we wake it up. Diago's cream can wake it up.

(They laugh. The Minister looks indignantly at the man.)

OFFSTAGE VOICE. Tim, what was that?

REPORTER, *still laughing.* Nothing. It seems an owner of a factory that produces hair revitalization cream tried to drum up business through the news. We have a circuslike atmosphere over here.

OFFSTAGE VOICE, *laughing.* He should pay for it. It's an ad, Tim.

REPORTER, *smiling.* Steve, listen. I've got good news here. Today is the kid's birthday. It comes two days before Christmas. So happy birthday to him and merry Christmas, everybody. *(To the Minister)* Thank you, Mr. Minister. Back to the studio.

(He leaves, followed by the cameraman and the crowd. A long pause. The Minister reflectively stares at the Old Woman, who is busy feeding the cat.)

MINISTER, *approaching Martin, kindly but carefully.* Martin, you've never invited me to your birthday.

(Light rises on Martin's face. A look of pain crosses his face. A sad, sweet melody is heard, first distantly and then growing closer while the area around the tree and Martin brightens.)

MARTIN. I will not go home, father.

MINISTER, *delicately, with a smile.* Will you invite me this time?

MARTIN, *with determination.* I will not go home.

(A long pause)

MINISTER, *in a very delicate, emotional tone.* Do you remember, son, when you came to the church and asked me to teach you how to ring the church bells? (A pause) I taught you. (With a compassionate smile) But you used to do it in a different way. (A slight pause) So sweet, though. Remember?

MARTIN. Yes, I do, father.

MINISTER, *carefully.* Did she like it?

MARTIN, *turning to him.* Who?

MINISTER. Mom. *(Then, after a considerable pause)* I understand, son. *(Quietly)* The world is easier to change than we think, Martin.

(The melody fades away. Light rises on the house. Professor Rex appears, descending the stairs of the house. He is wearing a long, colorful skirt. He indifferently looks at Martin and the Minister.)

MINISTER, *loudly, to Professor Rex.* Good evening, professor.

PROF. REX, *coldly.* Good evening.

MINISTER, *carefully.* Martin has just invited me to his birthday party tonight.

PROF. REX, *callously.* Oh, really?

(A long pause)

MINISTER, *approaching him discreetly.* How is teaching, Professor Rex?

PROF. REX. I'm not teaching anymore.

MINISTER. Why?

PROF. REX, *offhandedly.* The university fired me. I'm suing them now.

MINISTER. I'm awfully sorry to hear this. How do you keep yourself busy then?

PROF. REX. I am quite busy now. I am a photographer. *(A slight pause)* A nude photographer.

MINISTER, *stunned.* A nude photographer?

PROF. REX, *carelessly.* Yes. I don't mind being known as a nude photographer. I'm writing a book too.

MINISTER, *trying to maintain a neutral expression of polite interest.* Interesting! What is it about?

PROF. REX. Logotherapy and nude photography.

MINISTER, *suppressing a bitter smile.* Logotherapy and nude photography. A wonderful combination!

PROF. REX. It is. *(After a pause)* As a matter of fact, I am proposing a new theory.

MINISTER. Really?

PROF. REX. Well, I believe that since the beginning of life, man has been revealed as a being in search of meaning—a search whose futility seems to account for many of the ills of our age.

OLD MAN, *singing.* Mister, I call you mister, and you are my sister.

PROF. REX, *becoming enthusiastic.* In every human being, there is this unheard cry for meaning, which I believe devalues, debases, and depreciates what is really genuine, what is really genuinely human in man.

MINISTER. What is that?

PROF. REX, *in a cold, quiet tone.* The human body.

MINISTER, *sharply but contained.* The human body?

PROF. REX. Yes, the human body is the only possible beautiful meaning, and nude photography can help man realize this.

MINISTER, *unable to bear him.* Realize what?

PROF. REX, *in a colder tone.* I'll give you one example. Look at those gays and lesbians and the time they waste before they discover their sexual preferences. Nude photography helps man and woman unmask, value, and appreciate the beauty of the human body.

MINISTER, *exploding at him.* You want us to live like animals?

PROF. REX. In fact, animals were lucky, because they did not have the mind to mislead them into seeking what is beyond the human body. They were lucky because they started there, and I believe that we are on the way to it.

MINISTER, *furious.* To what?

PROF. REX, *with absolute assurance.* The happy transformation.

MINISTER, *with a great deal of controlled tension.* Wait, wait. Your conclusion is false because your premise is false, and ...

(Jackie enters from left. She is carrying two boxes for the birthday party. The bizarreness of her hairstyle is noticeable: it is buzzed on the sides, bleached out, and blue.)

PROF. REX, *turning to her with a joyful scream.* Oh, Jackie! *(Moving toward her, fascinated, looking at her hair)* Oh, it's fabulous!

JACKIE. You like it?

PROF. REX. You bet I do.

JACKIE. It took me all day to do it.

PROF. REX, *smiling.* Where did you get the time to do the other things? (Looking at her whole body in appreciation) They are all great! The whole thing is fabulous. Just fabulous!

JACKIE, *seductively.* Is Kate in?

PROF. REX. Of course. We'll have a great party. *(Turning to the Minister, in a careless tone)* Excuse me.

(Jackie moves toward the house followed by Prof. Rex.)

MINISTER, *decidedly and in a dominant tone to Prof. Rex.* Will you please tell her that I will come to say happy birthday to Martin?

PROF. REX, *turning to him indifferently.* Okay.

(Jackie and Prof. Rex enter the house.)

MINISTER, *worried and exhausted, moving toward Martin.* We go together, Martin.

MARTIN. I don't want to go, father.

MINISTER. This time for me. *(A pause)* But I want to prepare something before we go. It's freezing out here. Let's get into the church for a few minutes. (Kindly taking his arm) Please …

(They both enter the church.)

OLD MAN, *deliriously to the Old Woman.* It looks like we have a date! I mean you and I have a date!

OLD WOMAN, *still feeding the cat.* Go away. Go away. I got work to do. *(To the cat)* Now, listen to me, Nefr. *(A slight pause)* Your bed is wet, and I know you don't like it wet. Let me change it before you sleep, honey.

OLD MAN, *singing.* Everybody loves somebody, sometime. *(Stops.)* Sometime, some place. *(Turning to her)* Listen, why don't we have some fun now? Your place or my place. I mean here. *(A pause)* Let's have it now. You know, it gets more fun when you get older. *(In a serious tone)* You know why? *(A pause)* Because you get experience. I have it now. After sixty years of sex, I still love it, especially in winter. *(A slight pause)* You know, experience makes a difference. Everywhere you go, they ask you about the experience on your resume, and after those sixty years of sex, I've got wonderful experience. But I lost the job. Yeah, I lost the job.

OLD WOMAN, *shouting in anger.* Don't talk to me, insane.

OLD MAN. Why so nervous? Nothing to be nervous about. I know it's not decent for a lady to have it here on this park bench. But believe me, it's very comfortable here, and we can have it here. All of it here—I tell you it's very comfortable here. It's even soft. *(Sadly)* Yeah, softer than the human heart. It took me a long time to know that. I know it now. *(A pause)* But I'm not afraid anymore. Life doesn't scare me now, because I have my gun. Do you know why I have a gun? *(A slight pause)* Because I am a stray like your cat.

OLD WOMAN, *scared.* She is not a stray. She is an Egyptian mau. My son gave her to me on my birthday. She left home because her first babies died in the oven. She came here, and I made her this box. *(A slight pause)* She thinks it's safe here. *(Sadly, to the cat)* No, it's not safe here. I told you, Nefr.

OLD MAN, *singing.* You keep going your way,
and I keep going my way,
and you dirty, muddy river,
keep out of my way.

You dirty, muddy river,
keep out of my way.

(He stands up, slowly moves toward the tree, stops at it, and then gets down on his knees, looking closely at it.)

OLD WOMAN, *with dread*. What are you looking for?

OLD MAN. The sign.

OLD WOMAN. What sign?

OLD MAN. A leaf.

OLD WOMAN. At this time of the year?

OLD MAN. Yeah, I can't do it if it's not there.

OLD WOMAN. Do what?

OLD MAN. Take what I gave to life.

OLD WOMAN. You gave nothing, old fool.

OLD MAN. I should take it, though.

OLD WOMAN. Take what?

OLD MAN. Nothing. You said it. Nothing.

(The Minister and Martin reappear. They move toward the house. Martin is nodding affirmatively while listening attentively to the Minister.)

MINISTER. I'm really proud of you, Martin. But man should always have hope. Having hope means you have trust in God.

OLD MAN, *shouting after them*. Don't go, my son. Don't go to her. It's too late, too late.

MINISTER, *gently pulling Martin to him*. Don't listen to him. He's drunk.

(They both enter the house.)

OLD MAN, *desperate and tired, moving toward the bench.* You dirty, muddy river, keep away. *(Sits.)* Keep away. *(To the Old Woman)* You know, it will be a great party. They'll have a great time. Great fun! What do you say now? They're no better than us. Let's have it here, now. *(Shouting)* Here and now. Now or never. Let's have it. Don't you know it? Hey, come on, old woman. We're all here because we know it. *(Gives a small laugh.)* Don't I look sexy? Yeah, I don't look sexy. I know it. I know. You know, when I was young, I used to go to them. You know them? They told me I don't look sexy. But they were very helpful. In the middle of it, they used to say encouraging words like, oh good, oh terrific, so big. *(Solemnly)* In point of fact, it was not so big or that terrific. *(To himself)* Hey, come on, old man, you know we all need encouragement to work it out. We need a lie to do it. We all lie. *(Trying to sing)* Lie together; lie to each other. *(A pause)* To tell you the truth, I liked the lie. I wanted them to help me out—I mean help me in. *(Considering)* In the out. I like both. You know, you can't have this without the other. But what I liked most was the lie. I still like it. *(Turning to her)* Do you like it?

(She does not respond.)

OLD MAN. Turned you off? Yeah, I turned you off. Sorry. *(Stands up, slowly moves upstage, stops, looking at the house.)* Well, since we're not going to do it, (pointing to the house) let me see it there! *(He moves two steps toward the backyard of the house, then stops, turns, and stares at the sky. Then, to the sky) You have a minute? Not now—I know you're damn busy. (Listens) Oh, no, I don't want any changes in your schedule. You know, it will only take a minute. (Listens) Tonight? Perfect. Thank you. (He discreetly moves around to the backyard of the house, enters it, and disappears.)*

OLD WOMAN, *after making sure he is gone.* He's mad. I remember his face. I saw him here, but I don't remember when. His eyes scare me. He has a devil's face. I'm scared. *(To the cat)* I'm scared, Nefr. I told you it wouldn't be safe here. It's not safe. He's mad. You heard him say he has a gun. He wants me to let you die. What shall we do now? I can't leave you. I'm tired. I'm freezing. But

I can't leave you alone with him. I can't. We should not make the same mistake twice. *(With pain)* Remember when your first beautiful babies died? It was not my mistake. Believe me, Nefr. I'm old and sick. *(Sobbing)* I didn't mean it. It wasn't my mistake. It was nobody's mistake. But God wants us to learn. And I learned. I will not leave you, honey. *(She moves to the bench, sits, and wraps herself up. She is deeply worried and tired, but her face shines with wild determination. Loudly, to the cat)* I'm here, honey. Do not be afraid. I'm not going, baby.

(End of Act one)

ACT TWO

(Kate's living room. It is furnished with a few pieces of wood furniture. On the left toward the back, there is a window covered with heavy curtains. The Minister and Martin are sitting on separate occasional wood chairs beside the fireplace. The fire is lit. In front of them, Kate is sitting on a sofa, drinking by herself. Despite her erect and rigid appearance, her face reveals deep suffering. To the far left, Jackie and Prof. Rex are getting things ready for the party on a large occasional table covered with a cloth. Their crude laughter does not seem to dispel the tense atmosphere.)

PROF. REX, *crudely, laughing.* Jackie, how can you talk so dirty and keep your lips so shiny?

(Both give a loud, brutish laugh. The Minister tries to keep himself and Martin busy talking. Kate avoids looking at them and drinks.)

PROF. REX, placing the candles. Listen, you didn't tell me who is your best lover *(smiling demurely)* aside from your husband. *(They share a loud laugh.)* I know it's a difficult question. *(Looking at her hair)* Your hairstyle fascinates me. How did you do it?

JACKIE. Simple. You mix half an ounce of sugar with three ounces of water and apply it to your already wet hair with a spray bottle. Then—then you mix.

PROF. REX, *looking at her body.* Wonderful. The whole thing fascinates me. This is the real thing! The real meaning!

JACKIE. Yeah, I feel tremendously good about my body tonight. *(A pause)* It's hot here. *(Takes off her coat, revealing a topless dress.)* I feel I'm on fire here. *(Approaching him, in a low voice)* Listen, how about a little game with the father tonight?

PROF. REX. I guess he's not the type.

JACKIE. Come on, they're all Jimmy Swaggarts.

PROF. REX. Yeah, but he is slightly different.

JACKIE, *laughing.* Slightly!

(They laugh.)

PROF. REX, *loudly to all.* Okay. Everything is ready now. Martin, you come over here so you can blow out the candles. They are eleven. *(Gives a small laugh.)* It is not an easy job. Nobody will give you a hand.

(They all gather around the table.)

PROF. REX. Ready? Ten, nine, eight, seven, six, five, four, three, two, one. Go.

(Martin blows out the candles.)

MINISTER, *kissing him.* Happy birthday, son.

MARTIN. Thank you, father.

(The Minister steps behind Martin and puts his hands on Martin's head, waiting for Kate with a kind, suggestive look in his eyes. Kate moves toward Martin and embraces him, keeping him in her arms for a few seconds.)

KATE. Happy birthday, honey.

(The same sad, sweet flute melody is heard from afar.)

MARTIN, *holding her hands and looking passionately into her face.* Thank you, Mom.

(The melody fades out.)

JACKIE, *holding a bottle of wine.* My turn now, Martin. Do you remember the woman who poured perfume on Jesus' head? I have no perfume. I have this fine champagne. *(Pouring it on his head)* Happy birth—

MINISTER, *turning to her in fury.* Do not do that, woman.

JACKIE, *boldly.* Hey, you don't tell me what to do. You—

KATE, *screaming.* Shut up! Shut up, all of you, please. I'm sick and tired. Please.

(A long pause. Kate moves toward her sofa, sits, reaches for her glass.)

KATE, *trying to control her shaky hands and trembling voice.* Mr. Minister—let me call you Mr. Minister. I hate the word father. *(A pause)* I heard your comment in the news. It was moderate and *(looking for the word)* considerate, so to speak. I—

PROF. REX, *interrupting in a cold tone.* Not specific, though.

MINISTER, *turning to him, calmly.* How?

PROF. REX. You didn't specify the problem.

MINISTER. What is the problem?

PROF. REX, *defiantly looking at him.* You.

MINISTER, *furious.* Me?

PROF. REX. You're feeding the kid your stuff.

MINISTER, *fiercely.* Listen, I am not here to talk to you. You are not the right person. (Hesitates.) You are not the right person to talk to.

PROF. REX, *insulted.* Right person? What is that supposed to mean?

MINISTER, *avoiding him and turning to Kate, softly.* I am here to talk to you, madam. I am not going to preach or make a speech. *(Glancing at Jackie and Prof. Rex)* I am not going to talk about abnormalities. *(In a soft, pleading tone)* I am here to talk about Martin and you. *(After a pause)* Madam, it is impossible for Martin or any normal human being to adjust to what is going on here, and—

KATE, *interrupting with great tension.* Please, Mr. Minister., I don't want to talk about anything. You are my guest, and I thank you for your concern. *(Beginning to lose control over her voice)* But I do not want to talk about anything else, please.

MINISTER, *persistent, quiet.* I think you will be amazed to know that I have read your play. Yes. I have read your *Winter Dream.* Also, I have read all that you have said in your interviews. It was hard for me to get the materials, but I wanted to know. *(Taking a note out of his pocket)* I have read your play, madam, and I am not a literary critic to say it is good or bad. *(A slight pause, looking into her face)* But when I read the play, I discovered in your play and in you a part I can talk to. In your play, you say *(reads)* "Men envy women for that unquestionable love between them and their children." I am here to talk to this part in you. You say you write from your heart.

KATE, *after a long pause, trying to regain her erect and rigid appearance.* Yes, Mr. Minister, I write from my heart. But why do you take a part of my play and leave out the whole? Why does your damn society always take a part and leave out the whole? *(Facing him fiercely)* Why are you wearing a mask?

MINISTER, *calmly.* I am wearing no mask, madam. I have only the face you see now.

KATE, *almost screaming.* Your society's mask. The father's mask.

MINISTER, *shocked, confused.* I do not see what you mean!

KATE, *after a pause, gazing into the distance.* Twenty years ago, I started performing in San Francisco. I still remember that Christmas break when I went home and they told me he had killed himself.

MINISTER. Who?

KATE, *acidly.* My father. He went into the garage and shot himself. A lot of people know the story, but they don't know the big secret. *(Laughs a small, cutting laugh.)* They don't know why he killed himself. *(Turning to the Minister)* You know why? *(A pause)* Because he wanted to free me and himself. I guess you are curious to know from what? *(Frantic, agonized)* I was Daddy's favorite. No one knew it. Even my dumb mom didn't know it.

(Stunned silence)

KATE, *in a mad trance.* Daddy showed me what it's like to be a mama. I still remember the first time. I couldn't understand it. But I lived it. I lived it. And I couldn't say a word, because he was my daddy. *(Crying)* And nobody protected me. All my prophets, kings, princesses, and dollies couldn't protect me from my daddy, because he was my daddy. Yeah, my daddy. Then he killed himself to free me and himself. Yes, Daddy, you freed yourself but not me. Not me, Daddy. I lived with the scar on my body. *(Screaming in agony)* I lived with the scar on my body, Daddy. *(A pause)* I ran away to acting. I thought acting would be my rescue, my freedom from that part God has given me. But it was not. The scar got bigger and bigger till it became me. And I had to learn how to live with it. I started writing when I learned how to live with pain. I needed time. Time. *(A pause)* Time has shown me that I am not alone. There are thousands like me. Victims like me. Thousands, *(turning to the Minister)* you hear me?

MINISTER, *in sympathy and sorrow.* I am really sorry to—

KATE, *interrupting fiercely.* No, no. I don't want your sympathy. I don't need it. *(Daringly, looking into his face)* You say you found in my play and in me a part you can talk to. *(Ironically)* Not this time The game is over, father. Why do you talk to a part? Why don't you talk to the whole of me and my play? Why don't you talk to the scar that has become me, the headaches and illnesses that are all I have? Why don't you talk to the whole of me, my play, and your dead culture? *(A pause)* Can you tell me why they canceled my play? Sexual issues? Political issues? The combination?

MINISTER, *quietly.* Madam, now I understand—

KATE, *interrupting.* No. You didn't understand and you will never understand. But we will force you to understand. Someday, my play and all the victims' stories will be told. And you know where? *(A pause)* In your churches!

MINISTER. Why churches?

KATE. Because you created the lie there. The father's lie. We are going to unmask you—every father, father. You might take my body away, but you cannot take my soul—my spirit and my soul. I am not going to stop writing. You do not scare me anymore, father. *(Getting up, steadily)* Now, Mr. Minister, I want you to do me a favor. *(After a pause, facing him)* Please leave me and my son alone. Keep out of our life, please.

MINISTER, *standing, moving toward the door.* I will. But, before I go, I should tell you this. We know and see God by his signs, and you have his sign in your heart. It is your love for Martin. It is God's sign, and you cannot destroy it because it is indestructible. If you try, you will destroy yourself with it. You hear me? You will destroy yourself.

KATE, *shouting.* Leave us alone, please.

MINISTER, *holding the door, calmly.* I will. Good night. *(To Martin)* Good night, Martin.

(A long pause.)

JACKIE, *frustrated.* What shall we do now? What shall we do tonight?

PROF. REX, trying to cheer both of them up. Tonight?

JACKIE. Yeah.

PROF. REX, *seductively but coldly, looking at Kate and Jackie.* Tonight is like all our nights. *(With determination)* And it will be our best night. We will have fun. We will do everything we can imagine. *(Joyfully)* Yeah, there is a lot we can imagine. *(Looking at Martin, who looks agonized and frightened)* Yeah, tonight will be our best night.

(The scene changes into the scene of act one. Now the Old Woman is asleep on the bench. The Old Man reappears, coming from the backyard. He seems happy.)

OLD MAN, *moving downstage toward the bench, loudly to the Old Woman.* Hey, my princess, wake up. Wake up.

(She wakes up, startled and terrified.)

OLD MAN, *after a pause.* Wake up. There's a storm coming. A great storm. You better go home.

(She stands up, moves toward the box, and stops at the fence.)

OLD WOMAN, *scared.* Go. Go away.

OLD MAN. You love your cat so much? Yeah, you do. *(A pause)* I'll tell you a secret.

OLD WOMAN. Don't talk to me.

OLD MAN, *taking a drink.* No, I should tell you. I am going to tell only you. You know why? *(Laughs.)* Because you know it. So I should tell you.

OLD WOMAN. I don't want to hear it.

OLD MAN. You asked me who I am, and I should tell you. I am someone who lived all his life without love. But tonight I discovered that I can love. Yes, I can love. I can live. I can die. Love, live, and die. *(Looking at her)* They are all one, you know. Yes, they are all one. *(Singing)* We dreamers have our own ways of facing rainy days. Our own ways of facing rainy days. Rainy days …

> *When the sky looks so gray,*
> *I think of you.*
> *When the winter wind is too strong,*
> *I concentrate on you.*
> *I concentrate on you.*

(Looking at her) Yes, I can die now. But I want to laugh before I die. And it should be well played.

(Martin enters, rushing out of the house's door. He still has the Bible in his hand. He is in great agony.)

MARTIN, *loudly, moving upstage toward the tree.* No, Mom. I will not come back. I will never come back.

(Kate opens the living-room window, which looks on the park.)

KATE, *screaming, agonized.* Martin, come back! Please come back. Don't listen to him. He is like every father. He will deceive you. Come back, Martin. He is cheating on you. I am not cheating on you, because I am your mom. *(With great pain)* I am your mom. *(Crying)* I love you. I have always loved you. Yes, I love you. Please come back.

MARTIN, *sobbing.* I love you too, Mom. I love you. But I will never come back. *(Sits on the snow beside the tree.)* I love you, Mom. But he is not cheating on me. He has never cheated on me. He has never said a bad word about you to me.

KATE, *still crying in despair.* Please, Martin, come back.

(Martin stands up and turns his face toward the window.)

MARTIN, *shouting with determination.* Mom, you have never asked me about the nights I spent crying alone in my room. You have never asked me about the pains in my stomach. And I have no friends, Mom. I cannot invite them, and you know why. You have never listened to me, Mom. *(Loudly)* You have to listen now, Mom. *(A slight pause)* The devil is leading you and your friends. The devil knows exactly how to please you on the way to hell. Do you know the story of the man who dropped beans along the road to the slaughter for the pigs? They went on picking up the beans, never thinking they were going to the slaughter. This is your way, Mom. This is your way, Mom. But I don't want you go there, Mom. *(Sobbing)* Because you are my mom. I want you to turn to my way. *(A pause)* Your friends say I'll grow up and understand. But it hurts, Mom. *(Screaming in pain)* It hurts, Mom. I can see all women do what you and your friends do in front of me, but not you, Mom. Not you, Mom. It hurts and don't ask me why. Ask him—the creator. *(A pause)* You talk about me changing. To what, Mom? I have never seen you smile. And if your way hasn't brought you happiness, why don't you turn to my way, Mom?

Why? Why? I have never seen a smile on your face. But I have seen him in your face. *(Staring wildly)* I have seen the devil in your face, Mom. *(Choking with his pain and love)* And I am going to face him for you, Mom. *(Crying out his words)* I am going to fight him for you, Mom. I am going to fight for God's sign in you and me, Mom. I love you. You hear me? I love you. Turn to my way. Turn to me. Turn to me.

(Now the flute melody is heard. Martin hears the church bells ringing the way he used to ring them. The light rises on him and the tree.)

OLD MAN, *kindly, going to Martin.* You are right, son. You are right. They do not know. Yes, they do not know. But they will know. They will know when the tide is out. There will be a lot to discover when the tide is out.

MARTIN, *listening, gazing at the church.* You hear it?

OLD MAN. Yes, I do. It is beautiful. *(A pause)* And you should be happy, Martin. You should be happy, because your way is free now. Those who were against you, who tried to block your way, are defeated now. Yes, they are defeated. They are down.

(The Old Man moves toward the tree, stops, and kneels down, looking closely at it.)

MARTIN. Looking for the sign?

OLD MAN. Yes. I do not see it.

MARTIN. It is not there.

OLD MAN. I cannot do it, then.

MARTIN, *gazing at him, dazed, dreaming.* And if I give you the password?

OLD MAN, *getting up, looking at him.* What?

MARTIN, *after a pause.* I love you.

OLD MAN, *deeply moved, bewildered, approaching him.* I love you too, my son. I love you. *(Embraces him, crying and looking into his face)* I love you, Martin. *(He gently breaks loose from Martin, drifts off three steps, then turns to him.)* I love you. *(With great difficulty)* And I can do it now. *(Takes out his gun.)* Yes, I can do it now. *(He shoots Martin.)*

(The Old Woman gives a loud scream and stands petrified, gazing at Martin. The Old Man stands petrified too. Martin staggers toward the tree and, finally, embraces it while falling. The curtain falls.)

THE NEW ODYSSEY: A ONE-ACT PLAY

CHARACTERS

PROFESSOR ODYSSEUS

HESIOD

HOMER

SHAKESPEARE

HAMMER : A department assistant

(A spacious round room in the Department of Human Studies at Washington State University. The door is to the right of a chair set at the end of a table. To the left, there is a large mirror and many shelves crowded with books. Behind the table, there is a large screen occupying the whole background. It is at the most wretched hour between a black night and a wintry morning in the year 1999, when Professor Odysseus is sitting up. He is alone, absorbed in his thoughts. Suddenly, he seems determined and calls out.)

PROF ODYSSEUS. Hammer! Hammer!

HAMMER *coming.* Yes … yes, sir?

PROF. OD., *after a pause.* Are they all ready?

HAMMER. Yes, sir. Hesiod, Homer, and Shakespeare—all of them, but *(hesitating)* they are terribly terrified, and you seem tired. *(In sympathy)* Professor Odysseus, for long nights you have been here forgetting everything, and—

PROF. OD., *interrupting wearily.* Well, let them in.

HAMMER, *afraid.* Mrs. Odysseus is here. She is begging to come in.

PROF. OD., *with a dreadful, cold intensity.* No, no—I said no. This is my last resort, and today *(pensively dreaming)* should be the end.

HAMMER. The end! What end, sir?

PROF. OD., *aside.* I choose to make sense for those in the know; for those who are not, I choose to forget everything. *(To Hammer)* Well, have you sent the questions to the Future Room?

HAMMER. Yes, sir. This time they say there may be an answer.

PROF. OD. We hope so. Well, go then. Let Hesiod, Homer, and Shakespeare in.

(Hammer moves toward the door while Prof. Od. stands with his back to it. Shakespeare first appears, followed by Hesiod and Homer. Each glances around dazedly.)

PROF. OD., *suddenly facing them.* Welcome, sirs. Welcome. *(Pointing to the chairs)* Sit down. Welcome, Mr. Hesiod, the first who claimed to explain the formation of the universe.

HESIOD. Thank you, sir. *(Rising in amazement)* Is it possible—

PROF. OD., *interrupting, to Homer and Shakespeare, who look at him anxiously.* Welcome, Homer, the father of our great poets, and you, Shakespeare, the greatest dramatist as acknowledged by most scholars. *(A pause)* Welcome, all. *(Moves to the shelves, picking out three books.)* Of course you are bewildered about where, how, *(putting the books on the table)* and why you are here! But the whole thing will soon be clear. I am Professor Z. Odysseus, lecturer and critic at Washington State University, where you are now. You are here to save human life.

HESIOD. Save human life?

PROF. OD. Yes, human life is determined to disappear completely in a few months. Large parts of the world have already been destroyed after the Third World War, which began in the year 1995 and lasted five years. Well, that was not the last war. There is another one coming.

HESIOD. Another one coming?

PROF. OD. And it will be the end! *(After a pause)* Well, to save the rest, the World Council, formulated after that catastrophe, identified three professors who are believed to be the greatest able minds. One in the department of biology, one in the department of mathematics, and me. Everyone is to work separately, yet we are to find the cause and remedy so as to avoid the foretold end.

SHAKESPEARE, *hesitating.* I—I beg your pardon, sir. Of course we are quite willing to save man—but how?

PROF. OD., *agitated.* After much research and personal experience—yes, after personal experience—I have found the cause of destruction and misery in human life.

HESIOD. What is it, sir?

PROF. OD. I have realized that man's fault lies in that his scientific progress has not been accompanied by a similar one in his feelings. The human heart is still awfully lagging behind the mind, and *(after a long pause)* in women lies the defect, because when men desire women, they start to desire power—and death. Man is left now with two alternatives, either to go on waiting for death or to get rid of her.

HESIOD, *amazed*. Get rid of her?

PROF. OD., *determined*. Yes. This is the only way to save humanity.

HOMER, *hesitating*. May I ask, dear son, how we have come to be here? And in the year 1999—Mr. Hammer told us that we are in the year 1999!

PROF. OD. That is quite true.

HOMER. How then are we here?

PROF OD. A very important question. Man has become able now to recall images of the past. It is in his capacity also to see images of the future.

SHAKESPEARE. Images of the past and future?

PROF. OD. Yes, Mr. Shakespeare.

SHAKESPEARE. You mean to say we are images?

PROF. OD. Yes, and what you created are all real images.

HESIOD, *confused*. I beg your pardon, sir; I do not see what you mean.

PROF. OD. Well, we have discovered that all your characters—Prometheus, Penelope, Hamlet—all are real images that can be seen now. *(To Shakespeare, taking a bottle from one of the shelves)* Here you see the poison from which Gertrude died. Isn't it?

SHAKESPEARE, *going to him*. Yes ... yes, it is.

HESIOD, *curiously.* Professor Odysseus, you mean we can see Hamlet?

PROF. OD. Yes. Hamlet is there now.

ALL. Where?

PROF. OD. Here—I am Hamlet.

(All are shocked.)

HESIOD, *cunningly.* All right, sir, you said we are going to save human life by getting rid of women. How can that be done?

PROF. OD. This is possible—that is why you are here.

HESIOD. You mean ... *(terrified)* you mean we are going to take part in ...

PROF. OD., *convincingly.* And it is up to you, Mr. Hesiod, to start. *(He moves to the table while Hesiod rises in fear and amazement.)* Isn't this yours? *(Takes one of the three books on the table and reads.) The Theogony of Hesiod.* This was the first attempt, officially recognized, to explain the origin of life, the first image of man, the beginning. *(Moves to Hesiod, pleading.)* We implore you, for the sake of humanity—change it.

HESIOD, *shocked.* Change it? Change what, sir?

PROF. OD., *passionately.* The beginning—the origin of humanity. Isn't this yours? Isn't this yours? Isn't this yours? *(Reads.)* "But the astute Prometheus went to the island of Lemnos, where Hephaestus kept his forges. There he stole a brand of the holy fire which he enclosed in a hollow stalk and carried back to men ... and outraged by the theft, Zeus sent a fresh calamity to men ... women ... and with the arrival of the first woman, misery made its appearance on earth." *(Moves to Hesiod and takes him by the arms.)* Isn't that yours?

HESIOD, *giving up.* Yes—mine.

114

PROF. OD. Please change it. You have to change it if we want a different end!

HESIOD. All right, sir. Can you tell me how?

PROF. OD. Well, you can persuade Prometheus to steal something else.

HESIOD, *puzzled.* Steal something else?

PROF. OD. Why not the god himself? Why not bring the god down and kill him? Perhaps he might be the cause of all misery.

HESIOD, *frightened.* Believe me, sir, I can't. My *Theogony* was just a reflection of my time's beliefs. Believe me—what you ask is beyond my capacity.

PROF. OD., *thoughtfully.* Well, if he can't steal something else, let him give it back.

HESIOD. I can't, sir. I can't. Prometheus was made to steal fire—fire in particular—and woman was the punishment. Yes, she was the punishment.

(The door opens and Hammer comes in.)

HAMMER. Professor Odysseus, Mrs. Odysseus is outside. She says she doesn't know where to go.

PROF. OD., *angrily.* Tell her she can go where her eyes threaten me to go!

(Astounded, Hammer goes out.)

PROF. OD., *murmuring.* Yes, she can go where her eyes threaten me to. *(Disappointedly buries his head in his arms.)*

HOMER, *going to him, patting him on the shoulder.* Dear son …. dear son.

PROF. OD., *to Homer.* And you, old man, do you think you can deceive me with your image of Penelope, who set up a great loom in her palace and set to weaving a web of threads? Do you think she was waiting for her Odysseus? No. *(Agitated)* No! Isn't this yours? *(Takes the second book and reads.) The Odyssey*, book II: "for she holds out hope to all and makes promises to each man." *(Mournfully)* She holds out hope to all and makes promises to each man.

HOMER. But ... she explains this when she meets him in book XIX.

PROF. OD., *crying out.* No, she only justifies her crime!

HOMER. Her crime? My Penelope hasn't committed a crime!

SHAKESPEARE, *interrupting.* May we ask Professor Odysseus what kind of crime she has committed?

PROF. OD. The crime your Gertrude committed!

(Shakespeare and Homer, puzzled, look at each other.)

PROF. OD. You can't deceive me. You know quite well where is the disease, but you can't face it boldly. *(Takes the third book.)* Why? Why don't you face it boldly? *(To Shakespeare)* Why don't you let Hamlet kill his adulterous mother? Isn't this yours? *(Reads.)* "Taint not thy mind, nor let thy soul contrive against thy mother ought." *(Goes to Shakespeare.)* Why? What for?

SHAKESPEARE. But ... she dies.

PROF. OD. No, I said you can't deceive me. She dies only by chance. Why? What makes you so cowardly? Why? *(To Hesiod)* Would it be too expensive to get rid of her? Would not it be less expensive than what humanity has lost in wars? Why? *(To Shakespeare)* Why don't you ... *(Hesitates but suddenly takes Shakespeare by the arms.)* You know, Mr. Shakespeare. You know what Mr. Eliot says about your play, Hamlet. He—

SHAKESPEARE, *interrupting.* His objective correlative Oh, yes. But Eliot now, after coming to our land, has changed his mind.

PROF. OD. Your land? Changed his mind?

SHAKESPEARE. Sure. We real artists live in a separate land. It is the land of reality, and when Eliot joined us, we asked him to reread *Oedipus the King* and *Waiting for Godot* if he wanted to know.

PROF. OD. Know what?

SHAKESPEARE. Know that to be or not to be, to go or not to go, all are the same. Eliot now knows his mistake.

PROF. OD. His mistake?

SHAKESPEARE. And yours also.

PROF. OD., *amazed*. My mistake?

SHAKESPEARE. Yes. You trust life and words too much. That is why they have failed you. Life is incapable of giving that objective correlative, as he calls it. It is life's failure, not mine, and I have presented only life in that failure!

PROF. OD., *puzzled*. Mr. Shakespeare, you are still ambiguous. *(Pleading)* You say you real artists are living in a separate land of reality. Can I join you? I wrote two plays. I am not sure if they were good or not, but I feel I am a real artist. Can you—will you accept me?

SHAKESPEARE. No. As long as you live, you are allowed only to learn by suffering.

PROF. OD. Learn by suffering? *(Desperately)* But human life will soon come to an end. *(Frantically)* Can't you help me? Help the human race? Save humanity? You great coward!

HESIOD, *remonstrating*. No, sir, we are not cowards. We are only helpless.

(The door opens, and Hammer appears.)

HAMMER. Professor Odysseus, the answer to the question you sent to the Future Room will be able to be seen on the screen after three minutes.

PROF. OD., *joyfully*. Excellent! *(Going to Shakespeare)* You still can help me.

SHAKESPEARE. How, sir?

PROF. OD. The answer is coming now on the screen, and you, the master of images, can say what it means.

(The stage becomes dark, and the figures of Prof. Od., Hesiod, Homer, Shakespeare, and Hammer can hardly be distinguished. Light appears slowly on the screen.)

PROF. OD. What appears? See! See! Fire—fire fills up the whole screen. See! Penelope is coming out of the flames, still holding the loom, weaving her web. See! *(Horrified)* See! The threads are shedding blood. Oh, *(crying)* blood everywhere ... oh, threads dripping blood. See! These pale human faces ... oh, Orestes, Hamlet. Look—look, the other flames—Clytemnestra, Gertrude! Oh, blood! See! Threads ... blood ... blood ... back again ... human faces mourning ... questioning and despairing ... Still she is weaving threads of blood. *(Wailing)* Didn't Odysseus come back? Didn't Odysseus come back? Oh ... oh ...

(The image disappears, and light comes back to the stage. Hesiod, Homer, and Shakespeare are not there, while Prof. Odysseus, unaware of Hammer, has his head buried in his hands.)

PROF. OD. And even if he comes back, he will never get home. *(Madly)* Never ... never get home ... never get home.

HAMMER. Professor Odysseus, dear sir, Mrs. Odysseus wants to see you.

PROF. OD. No. Tell her she can go where her eyes threaten me to.

HAMMER. I told her, sir, but she says she doesn't know where to go.

PROF. OD. No, she knows, and I know she knows. She didn't say it, but I have known the heart ... I have known the eyes already, known them all. *(Dreaming)* Ask her about the corpse she planted in the garden!

HAMMER, *terrified.* The corpse?

PROF. OD., *crying.* Get out ... get out.

(Hammer leaves, and Prof. Odysseus is alone.)

PROF. OD. Ask her. Has it begun to sprout? Will it bloom this year? Tell her keep the dog far hence, because *(crying)* he is friend to man or ... with his nails he'll dig it up again. Oh, oh! *(Wailing and falling on his knees)* Unreal city ... unreal city.

(Slowly, the background fades in to show a turbulent sea. Large swells and the cries of men are heard from afar.)

PROF. OD. O my great father Odysseus, I hear you. I know the hour has come, and it is time to get home.

(He moves slowly to disappear gradually into the background. The curtain falls.)